ROSE GUIDE TO
EXODUS

R SE
PUBLISHING

Rose Guide to Exodus
© 2024 Rose Publishing

Published by Rose Publishing
An imprint of Tyndale House Ministries
Carol Stream, Illinois
www.hendricksonrose.com

ISBN 978-1-4964-8459-8

Some chapters adapted from *Life of Moses* (Rose Publishing, 2011), *The Exodus* (Rose Publishing, 2019), *The Tabernacle* (Rose Publishing, 2013), *Ark of the Covenant* (Rose Publishing, 2020), *Feasts of the Bible* (Rose Publishing, 2011), and *The Ten Commandments* (Rose Publishing, 2006).

Photos used under license from Shutterstock.com. Relief maps by Michael Schmeling, www.aridocean.com.

Printed in China by APS
April 2024, 1st Printing

CONTENTS

CHAPTER 1

Moses and the Exodus

About four hundred years before the exodus, Jacob with his sons and their families migrated from Canaan to Egypt to escape a famine. Jacob's son Joseph had become the most important ruler in Egypt after the pharaoh, and he made sure his family was well taken care of in Egypt.

Following Joseph's death, the descendants of Jacob (called Hebrews or Israelites) continued to thrive in Egypt. But eventually, Egypt's pharaohs forgot Joseph and enslaved the Hebrews. To prevent the Hebrews from further population growth, one pharaoh ordered that every newborn Hebrew boy was to be thrown into the Nile River!

It was during this time that a Hebrew named Moses was born. Drawn out of the Nile by Pharaoh's daughter, Moses grew up as a member of Pharaoh's household. But God had chosen Moses for something much greater than the Egyptian royal court. Years later, out of a burning bush on a mountainside, God called Moses to lead the Hebrew slaves out of Egypt, far from Pharaoh's grip.

The exodus is the story of God's deliverance of the Israelites from slavery in Egypt and into the land promised to Abraham, Isaac, and Jacob. It is an epic story with nightmarish plagues, amazing miracles, a face-off between divine powers, and a perilous journey through the wilderness. But at its heart, it is a story about a sovereign God who relentlessly protects and provides for those who trust in him and follow where he leads.

THE NAME MOSES

The Hebrew name Moses sounds similar to the Hebrew verb for "to draw out." Pharaoh's daughter named the child Moses because she "drew him out of the water" (Ex. 2:10).

But the name Moses has an Egyptian meaning as well and is found within other Egyptian names: Ramesses, Thutmose, and Ahmose. The first part of each of these three names is related to an Egyptian deity: Ra, Thut, and Ah. The second part of each name (messes/mose) means "boy" or "son."

WHO WAS MOSES?

Moses was perhaps the most important person in the Old Testament. His life was bound to the life of God's people and to God himself. In a special way, Moses represented the Israelites to God and God to the Israelites.

Moses was …

- ✠ a baby in danger of death who became a liberator of slaves;

- ✠ a man who disliked the limelight but became a national leader;

- ✠ an eighty-year-old shepherd who left his home and went to face a mighty pharaoh;

- ✠ a man slow of speech who became a prophet of God; and

- ✠ a husband and father who became a priest to thousands.

The life of this man changed the life of a nation-to-be.

> Since then, no prophet has risen in Israel like Moses, whom the LORD knew face to face, who did all those miraculous signs and wonders the LORD sent him to do in Egypt—to Pharaoh and to all his officials and to his whole land. For no one has ever shown the mighty power or performed the awesome deeds that Moses did in the sight of all Israel.
>
> DEUTERONOMY 34:10–12

THE BIRTH OF MOSES

In that time when the Hebrew people suffered under the yoke of slavery and death, Moses was born. Although Pharaoh had intended to destroy the Hebrews and frustrate God's plans to bless them, God worked through the most unexpected people to save the child Moses.

Moses's mother set him in a basket in the Nile River in a place where he would be found; and he was, by Pharaoh's own daughter! Moses's sister (most likely Miriam) wisely talked Pharaoh's daughter into giving the baby back to his mother to nurse him. In contrast to Pharaoh's evil intentions, his own daughter's tender and compassionate heart became a tool for baby Moses's salvation.

The child Moses was born to a slave family, rescued by a noble person, nurtured by his own slave mother, and educated as a member of the Egyptian nobility.

As we read the story of Moses's birth and rescue, we understand that God was working behind the scenes. In fact, Moses's own infant story anticipates what was about to happen to all of God's people later in the story of the exodus.

MOSES	ISRAEL
Moses came out of the Nile River miraculously "reborn" (Ex. 2:10).	Israel miraculously came out of the Red Sea as a people with a new identity (Ex. 14:21–22).
Moses became aware of injustice and responded (Ex. 2:11–12).	God heard the suffering of his people, and he acted decisively (Ex. 3:7–10).
Moses had to flee from Pharaoh's anger into the wilderness (Ex. 2:15).	Israel had to flee from Pharaoh's army into the wilderness (Ex. 14:8–9).
Moses met God at the burning bush on Mount Sinai (Ex. 3:1).	Israel met God while camping around the base of Mount Sinai (Ex. 19:1–2).
Moses, an Egyptian, became the deliverer of some troubled shepherds (Ex. 2:16–19).	God chose Moses, the shepherd, to deliver his people from Egypt (Ex. 3:1, 10).

DIVINE APPOINTMENT

In a burst of anger, Moses killed an Egyptian whom he witnessed beating a Hebrew slave. At that moment his life changed radically. After being an Egyptian noble, Moses became a fugitive. He fled into the wilderness and began a new life. In Midian, he established a new home, a new clan, a new profession as a shepherd, and he married and had children.

> Moses agreed to stay with the man [in Midian], who gave his daughter Zipporah to Moses in marriage. Zipporah gave birth to a son, and Moses named him Gershom, saying, "I have become a foreigner in a foreign land."
>
> EXODUS 2:21–22

Meanwhile, back in Egypt, the pharaoh Moses had known had died, but another equally ruthless pharaoh took his place. Still in slavery, the Hebrew people cried out to God under their burdens. The book of Exodus notes that God entered the scene directly: he listened, remembered, and acted in favor of his people.

> The Israelites groaned in their slavery and cried out, and their cry for help because of their slavery went up to God. God heard their groaning and he remembered his covenant with Abraham, with Isaac and with Jacob.
>
> EXODUS 2:23–24

God called out to Moses from a burning bush on Mount Sinai. God identified himself as the God of Moses's forefathers. In reverence, Moses removed his sandals because God's presence made the ground holy. God announced that he had seen his people's misery and was sending Moses to bring them out of Egypt. When Moses protested that he was not the right person for the job, God offered signs that he would be with him:

✠ Israel would worship God on the same mountain (Ex. 3:12).

✠ God revealed his own name to Moses (Ex. 3:14).

✠ God would perform great wonders (Ex. 3:20).

✠ Israel would not leave Egypt empty-handed (Ex. 3:21).

✠ God showed his power by changing Moses's staff into a snake (Ex. 4:2–4).

✠ God made Moses's hand leprous and immediately restored it back to health (Ex. 4:6–7).

Moses's encounter with God at the burning bush revealed much about God, Moses, and the Israelites:

✠ God is faithful to his promises; he had not forgotten his covenant with Abraham.

✠ God chose and equipped Moses to be his special representative.

✠ Moses's role became defined as that of an intermediary between God and Israel. From this moment on, Moses spoke to God on behalf of the Israelites and to the Israelites on behalf of God.

Moses in front of the burning bush

THE "I AM"

When God revealed his identity to Moses, God used a form of the Hebrew verb for "to be," calling himself "I Am Who I Am," or "I Will Be Who I Will Be," or simply "I Am."

> God said to Moses, "I AM WHO I AM. This is what you are to say to the Israelites: 'I AM has sent me to you.'"
>
> EXODUS 3:14

This name—this "I Am"—consists of only four Hebrew letters, all consonants, and in English, they would be YHWH. Interestingly, the ancient Hebrew alphabet is composed entirely of consonants—no vowels. It would not be until about 3,000 years after the first Hebrew books of the Bible were written that vowel points—a system of dashes and dots—would be introduced into the written language to indicate the vowel sounds.

יהוה

To emphasize God's holiness, when God's people read the Hebrew Scriptures, they would substitute a different name for God rather than vocalize the personal name of YHWH. They would say "Adonai," which means "Lord." They did this because they held the person of God in such reverence that they dare not speak his name.

In fact, God's name of YHWH is so holy and so much greater than every other name that the Jewish people did not even record the vowel sounds of the name just in case someone would accidentally correctly utter the name. Instead, Medieval rabbis substituted vowel sounds for the name Adonai. So, precisely how to pronounce the YHWH correctly is a little mysterious, because the name was not vocalized for centuries and the vowels in the written form were borrowed from another name for God. Because of this, for many years it was thought that the pronunciation of YHWH was "Jehovah," but the most up-to-date research indicates the most likely pronunciation is closer to "Yahweh."

CLASH OF THE GODS

When Moses returned to Egypt to see Pharaoh, he confronted a person whom the Egyptians considered a divinity. Pharaoh was seen as the "son of Ra" and a god of Egypt who was responsible for maintaining cosmic order and control on the earth. In the eyes of the Egyptians, it would seem that a foreign god of the Hebrews was challenging their own god, Pharaoh. A clash of the gods was the natural result.

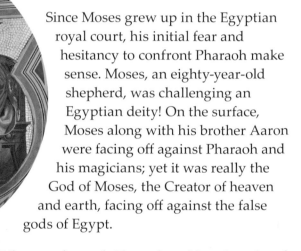

Since Moses grew up in the Egyptian royal court, his initial fear and hesitancy to confront Pharaoh make sense. Moses, an eighty-year-old shepherd, was challenging an Egyptian deity! On the surface, Moses along with his brother Aaron were facing off against Pharaoh and his magicians; yet it was really the God of Moses, the Creator of heaven and earth, facing off against the false gods of Egypt.

Moses confronts Pharaoh

When confronted, Pharaoh stubbornly refused to allow his Hebrew slaves to leave the country. He also worsened their conditions by denying them the straw needed to make bricks, causing it to be much more difficult to meet their quotas.

The Scriptures tell us that God was also behind Pharaoh's hardened heart. Pharaoh's obstinacy happened so that Moses and the Israelites would know that the Lord, the God of Abraham, Isaac, and Jacob, was the real and only God.

> I have raised you [Pharaoh] up for this very purpose,
> that I might show you my power and that my name might be
> proclaimed in all the earth.
>
> EXODUS 9:16

The Ten Plagues

As God performed signs and wonders across the land, the Egyptians, Moses, and the Hebrews witnessed God's power over all things. God revealed his sovereignty and ignited his people's faith by showing that he is the God ultimately in control.

> When the Israelites saw the mighty hand of the LORD displayed against the Egyptians, the people feared the LORD and put their trust in him and in Moses his servant.
>
> EXODUS 14:31

Exodus 12:12 states that God's judgment through the tenth plague came upon "all the gods of Egypt" (also Num. 33:4). Archaeologists are not certain about which particular deities were being worshiped in Egypt during the time of the exodus. Much of the information about Egyptian gods actually comes from a different time period and location in Egyptian history. Despite this uncertainty, it is still beneficial to consider possible connections between the ten plagues and Egyptian deities.

PLAGUE	DESCRIPTION	EGYPTIAN GODS
Water into Blood Ex. 7:14–25	The Nile River was turned into blood. This was the primary source of water in the land and the heart of Egyptian life.	**Hapi:** god of the annual flooding of the Nile **Khnum:** god of the source of the Nile
Frogs Ex. 8:1–15	Frogs invaded everything, eventually dying and unleashing foul smells throughout the land.	**Heqet:** goddess of fertility and childbirth, represented as a frog

PLAGUE	DESCRIPTION	EGYPTIAN GODS
Gnats/Lice Ex. 8:16–19	Dust turned into small insects, possibly gnats or lice. The Egyptian priests could not duplicate this plague.	**Geb:** god of the earth; gnats came from the "dust of the earth."
Flies/Mosquitoes Ex. 8:20–32	The precise identity of these flying insects is unclear. Psalm 78:45 suggests that the insects fed on the Egyptians.	**Khepri:** god of the rising sun, represented with the head of a fly or scarab beetle
Death of Livestock Ex. 9:1–7	A plague was sent on the Egyptian livestock in the fields. The Israelites' livestock was unharmed.	**Hathor:** mother and sky goddess, represented by a cow **Apis:** pictured as a bull sacrificed and reborn
Boils Ex. 9:8–12	Boils appeared on both the Egyptians and their animals. Egyptian priests/healers could do nothing to help.	**Imhotep:** god of healing and medicine **Sekhmet:** goddess of healing

PLAGUE	DESCRIPTION	EGYPTIAN GODS
Hail Ex. 9:13–35 	A massive hailstorm struck Egyptian lands. Some of Pharaoh's officials sided with Moses after this plague.	**Seth:** god of storms and disorder **Nut:** goddess of the sky
Locusts Ex. 10:1–20 	Locusts ate every plant not destroyed in the hailstorm. Egyptian officials pleaded with Pharaoh to listen to Moses.	**Serapia:** god with the head of a locust who protected against locusts
Darkness Ex. 10:21–29 	Intense darkness descended upon the land for three days; so dark that it was described as if it could be touched.	**Ra, Amon-ra, Atum, Horus:** gods associated with the sun
Death of Firstborn Sons Ex. 11:1–12:30 	God struck dead all firstborn males, including Pharaoh's son. But those with lamb's blood on their doorframes were spared (Passover).	This plague was an attack on the lineage and deity of Pharaoh himself.

Signs and Wonders or Natural Events?

Some people try to connect the cause of the plagues to natural events rather than supernatural occurrences. The turning of the water into blood has been linked to the Nile River becoming high during the months of July and August and turning "bloodlike" because of the red earth stirred up from the basins of the Blue Nile and Atbara. The result of this unusually high and muddy river could have caused the migration of frogs out of the river, leading to gnats and flies, which in turn led to disease and cattle deaths, and possibly even boils on humans. Other plagues have been tied to a weather disaster that could have resulted in what is described as a hailstorm and the swarming of locust, which was followed by a dust storm that caused the sun to be blocked out. While some of these explanations sound plausible, they cannot explain everything, like the water turning into blood in other water sources (Ex. 4:9; 7:19). Also, there is no explanation given for the death of firstborn sons.

A NEW PEOPLE

The Lord said that in the tenth plague the firstborn males of every household would die unless the doorframe of that house was covered with the blood of a perfect lamb. On the night of the plague, the Lord "passed over" the homes with lamb's blood on the doorframes. This was the first Passover. The Passover was to be commemorated annually throughout the generations of Israel as a memorial forever. It was a new time of remembrance for a new nation, starting in Nisan (Aviv), the first month of their new religious calendar (Lev. 23:4–5).

After the death of his son, Pharaoh was a broken man and finally allowed the Israelites to leave Egypt. As God had promised, they left with an abundance of Egyptian silver, gold, and clothing (Ex. 3:21–22; 12:35–36).

But Pharaoh quickly changed his mind.

> When the king of Egypt was told that the people had fled, Pharaoh and his officials changed their minds about them and said, "What have we done? We have let the Israelites go and have lost their services!" So he had his chariot made ready and took his army with him.
>
> EXODUS 14:5–6

With a column of fire separating them, Pharaoh's troops trapped Israel against the Red Sea. Moses took charge in the midst of the people's doubts and fears. God promised to fight for them. As they crossed the sea in a mighty miracle of deliverance, a new people was born: God's people, a nation in formation.

Just as baptism symbolizes a new beginning in the life of a Christian, the crossing of the sea was a new beginning for Israel (see 1 Cor. 10:1–2). Pharaoh's army disappeared as the waters closed in on them. God's deliverance was complete.

The destruction of Pharaoh's army

A NEW RELATIONSHIP

Through the exodus experience, God created a people for himself. In time, he started a relationship with this people that would define the rest of God's involvement with humanity. Christ's work on the cross is the miracle that brings salvation and defines believers as a new people. The writer of the book of Hebrews explains: "This salvation, which was first announced by the Lord, was confirmed to us by those who heard him. God also testified to it by signs, wonders and various miracles, and gifts of the Holy Spirit distributed according to his will" (Heb. 2:3–4).

DIVINE PRESENCE IN THE WILDERNESS

As God's people moved away from the sea toward Sinai, they rejoiced for their liberation, but also grumbled and complained against Moses and Aaron, and then they disobeyed God's instructions.

They asked for the basics for life: food and water. God provided these in miraculous ways. For food, God gave them manna and quail. As for the water, God instructed Moses to strike a rock to give water to the Israelites. Even after seeing God's providence over and over, the Israelites doubted and asked the question that highlights a central issue in the books of Exodus through Deuteronomy: "Is the LORD among us or not?" (Ex. 17:7).

God's revelation to Moses on Mount Sinai (both in Exodus 3 and 19) established that God's presence was indeed with Moses. The battle against the Amalekites in Exodus 17 also shows that God's presence with Moses represented God's presence with the Israelites. When Moses held his staff above his head, the Israelites defeated the Amalekites. When Moses lowered his arms to rest them, the fate of the battle turned against Israel. This event illustrated Moses's intercession in favor of Israel and God's response to him.

When the Israelites arrived at the foot of Mount Sinai, God made it clear that his demonstration of power—the thunder, lightning, and the thick cloud—had a specific purpose: "So that the people will hear me speaking with you and will always put their trust in you" (Ex. 19:9). Moses

Sinai mountains

represented God to the people of Israel. God's presence with Moses was a sign for the people to know that God was with them as well. Moses's authority and guidance represented God's own authority and guidance.

God's presence with Moses remained the sign of divine presence until the tabernacle was built. The tabernacle, a portable "tent of meeting," became the visual representation of God's presence in the midst of his people. The Lord instructed Moses:

> Then have them make a sanctuary for me, and I will dwell among them. Make this tabernacle and all its furnishings exactly like the pattern I will show you.
>
> EXODUS 25:8–9

In a late Jewish tradition, the term *shekinah* became associated with God's presence. *Shekinah* is derived from a Hebrew word that means "dwelling." God's presence, the *shekinah,* in the wilderness was represented by a cloud during the day and the column of fire at night.

THE COVENANT AT SINAI

In Scripture, the wilderness is a symbol of the chaos and lifeless forces that oppose God. For the Israelites, it became a training ground for learning what it meant to be a people of God living in his presence.

God is holy, whereas the Israelites (and all humanity) lived with many impurities and sin. How could people live in the presence of a holy God? For the purpose of teaching Israel how to live as God's people in his presence and in the promised land, God gave Moses the Ten Commandments. These ten laws can be seen as a summary of the agreement (covenant) that God made with Israel at Sinai. Israel agreed to keep (obey) the terms of their agreement (stipulations of the covenant) and God agreed to be their God and King to bless, protect, and provide for them.

The covenant at Sinai became the basis for God's relationship with Israel. Moses was a kind of mediator of this covenant. When he climbed the mountain, he was representing the Israelites before God. When he descended the mountain, Moses was representing God to the people.

> Moses went back and summoned the elders of the people and set before them all the words the Lord had commanded him to speak. The people all responded together, "We will do everything the Lord has said." So Moses brought their answer back to the Lord.
>
> EXODUS 19:7–8

In the Mosaic covenant, God inscribed the words of the covenant on stone. Israel was to treasure them and keep them close to their hearts and minds forever. Their entire life should have been determined by these words. But humans are forgetful and rebellious. The Israelites broke the terms of the agreement on repeated occasions. For that reason, God had promised to instead inscribe his law in people's hearts (Deut. 30:6). He would send a perfect mediator of a new covenant, the Messiah (Heb. 9:15).

JESUS AS THE MEDIATOR

Sin separates humans from God. In Old Testament times, people related to God indirectly, through covenants, sacrifices, and human intercessors, such as priests and prophets. In the New Testament, Jesus as the perfect priest and prophet became the only mediator needed. As a prophet, he communicated God's will through his teachings and ministry (Heb. 1:1–2). As a priest, he offered the only perfect sacrifice that could bring people back to God (Heb. 10:10–14). The letter to the Hebrews makes it clear that Jesus is a mediator like Moses but superior to him: "Christ is the mediator of a new covenant, that those who are called may receive the promised eternal inheritance—now that he has died as a ransom to set them free from the sins committed under the first covenant" (Heb. 9:15). Paul explains that "there is one God and one mediator between God and mankind, the man Christ Jesus" (1 Tim. 2:5).

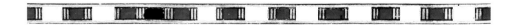

WANDERING IN THE WILDERNESS

God's people camped at the foot of Mount Sinai, and there they learned what it meant to be God's people and how to live with his holy presence in their midst; most of the instructions in the book of Leviticus are for exactly this purpose.

Organized as an army, Israel then traveled from Sinai to the edge of the promised land of Canaan. God, as their king, led the march through the wilderness and dwelt in the middle of their camp. At different times during the journey, both the people and Moses rebelled and expressed their discontent.

The Twelve Spies

As the Israelites approached the promised land, God instructed Moses to send twelve men to explore the land. Their report confirmed all that God had promised: a land flowing with milk and honey! However, they also brought bad news: the people in the land were strong and powerful! Filled with fear, and despite assurances from Moses, Joshua, and Caleb, the people rebelled and refused to follow God's instructions to conquer the land.

> All the Israelites grumbled against Moses and Aaron, and the whole assembly said to them, "If only we had died in Egypt! Or in this wilderness! Why is the LORD bringing us to this land only to let us fall by the sword? Our wives and children will be taken as plunder. Wouldn't it be better for us to go back to Egypt?"
>
> NUMBERS 14:2–3

After everything they had witnessed—freedom from slavery, the unexplainable plagues, the parting of the sea, food and water from divine miracles—still, they grumbled and mistrusted God.

God's punishment was terrible: that whole generation would die in the wilderness. The Israelites remained in the wilderness for forty years. Joshua and Caleb, the two faithful spies who trusted God, were the only two from that generation who would enter the promised land.

Why Didn't Moses Enter the Promised Land?

Moses had a unique relationship with God. When the Israelites grumbled and complained, they rebelled against God's authority. When Moses took his grievances to God, it was done in the context of a secure relationship and friendship. Because God treated Moses as a friend, Moses could appeal to God's own promises and honor (for example, Ex. 32:11–13; Num. 14:13–19). This forces us to wonder why God punished Moses (and his brother Aaron) so severely.

> But the LORD said to Moses and Aaron, "Because you did not trust in me enough to honor me as holy in the sight of the Israelites, you will not bring this community into the land I give them."
>
> NUMBERS 20:12

The Scriptures make it clear that Moses did something that offended God; something so serious that God refused him entry into the promised land: "You broke faith with me in the presence of the Israelites at the waters of Meribah Kadesh in the Desert of Zin and because you did not uphold my holiness among the Israelites" (Deut. 32:51). Here is what happened:

> [Moses] and Aaron gathered the assembly together in front of the rock and Moses said to them, "Listen, you rebels, must we bring you water out of this rock?" Then Moses raised his arm and struck the rock twice with his staff. Water gushed out, and the community and their livestock drank.
>
> NUMBERS 20:10–11

What was his sin? How did Moses break faith with God? These are some possible answers:

✠ Moses's speech to the Israelites may have been the offense. God commanded Moses to speak to the rock—not the people (Num. 20:8, 10).

✠ Moses may have been claiming for himself the miracle that he was about to perform: "Must *we* bring you water out of this rock?" (Num. 20:10, emphasis added).

✠ Moses was supposed to speak to the rock, not strike it.

✠ Moses's sin may have been a combination of the above reasons—or perhaps something not even recorded in Numbers 20.

How exactly did Moses's action show lack of trust and failure to give honor to God? Let us remember that God performed a similar miracle before in Exodus 17:1–7. There, at the rocky wilderness of Sinai, the people quarreled with Moses and asked for water. God ordered Moses to use his staff to strike the rock. Before the elders of the Israelites, Moses struck the rock and water came gushing out. In Numbers 20, the need for water arose once again. This time, however, God ordered Moses to speak to the rock.

Moses's sin might be a question of expectations. The people expected God to deliver them from their thirst in the same way he had done it before. Perhaps giving the Israelites water by speaking to the rock was a miracle they were not expecting; such a miracle could have had a stronger effect on their faith. By repeating the way the miracle was done previously, Moses, in a way, "robbed" glory from God's miraculous provision. Preventing God from acting in new and sometimes surprising ways may reflect a lack of faith and trust in God's goodness and wisdom. We cannot put God in a box; God is and does far more than we can imagine.

PROVISION, JUDGMENT, AND PRESENCE

The exodus journey—from the escape from Egypt to decades in the wilderness—is filled with examples of God teaching this new nation forming in the desert what it meant to be the people of God.

The exodus events include stories of God's judgment upon the people because of their grumbling and disobedience. Yet despite their lack of trust and frequent complaints, God demonstrated his faithfulness to his promises and provided for their needs. He also manifested his presence among them to build up the faith of this budding nation.

EVENT	GOD'S PROVISION
Ten Plagues Ex. 7–12	God delivered the Israelites from Pharaoh's oppression through signs and wonders. As they left, they plundered the Egyptians (Ex. 12:36).
Parting of the Sea Ex. 14:10–31	God parted the waters, allowing the Israelites to pass through on dry ground. The pursuing Egyptian army was destroyed by God as the waters collapsed.
Water at Marah Ex. 15:22–26	The water that the Israelites found at Marah was bitter. God showed Moses wood to throw in the water, and the water became drinkable.
Manna and Quail Ex. 16:1–36	The Israelites grumbled about their lack of food, so God provided quail for meat and manna, a white flaky substance appearing like dew in the morning.
Water from a Rock Ex. 17:1–7	The Israelites complained about their lack of water, so God told Moses to strike a rock with his staff, and water flowed from the rock.
Battle with Amalekites Ex. 17:8–16	While traveling to Mount Sinai, the Israelites were attacked by the Amalekites. God provided them victory in battle.
Ten Commandments, Covenant, Law Ex. 19:5–8; 20:1–17	In the covenant at Sinai, Israel agreed to obey God's law and God agreed to provide blessing, protection, and provision. Observing the law made it possible for a sinful people to live with a holy God.
Water from a Rock Num. 20:1–13	God told Moses to speak to a rock and it would produce water. Moses struck the rock instead. God still provided water despite Moses's disobedience.
Victory over Enemies Num. 21:1–3, 21–35	God provided the Israelites victory over their enemies as they approached Canaan. This secured land for them and sent fear into the surrounding nations.
Balaam's Blessings Num. 22:2–38	God caused Balaam to bless Israel instead of curse them as Balaam had been hired to do.

EVENT	GOD'S JUDGMENT
Golden Calf Ex. 32:1–35	Moses destroyed the golden calf idol and sent the Levites throughout the camp killing all who would not abandon their idolatry.
Fire in the Camp Num. 11:1–3	The Israelites were complaining so much that God's anger burned against them, and he sent a fire that burned the outer part of their camp.
Quail and Plague Num. 11:4–34	The Israelites grumbled again; this time over food. So God sent them quail from the sea. However, upon eating the meat, God struck the people with a plague killing those who had been complaining.
Miriam's Disease Num. 12:1–16	God defended Moses after Miriam and Aaron talked badly about him. He punished Miriam with a disease that turned her skin white like snow (leprosy). God restored her after seven days.
Refusal to Enter Canaan Num. 14:20–35	God punished the faithless Israelites by stating that all men twenty and older (except Caleb and Joshua) would die in the wilderness. After forty years had passed, their children would enter the promised land.
Korah's Rebellion Num. 16:1–50	God caused the earth to swallow up the leaders of a rebellion. The other 250 rebels were struck down by fire from God. The remaining Israelites blamed Moses, so God sent a plague that killed 14,700 people.
Disobedience Num. 20:1–13	Moses and Aaron were denied entry into the promised land for not honoring God.
Bronze Snake Num. 21:4–9	God punished the grumbling Israelites by sending venomous snakes. God then had Moses construct a bronze image of a snake on a pole for people to look at if they were bitten, so they would be healed.
Worship of Baal Num. 25:1–18	God instructed Moses to have all the men killed who were worshiping the false god Baal. God also sent a plague upon the Israelites.

EVENT	GOD'S PRESENCE
Pillars of Cloud and Fire Ex. 13:21–22; Num. 9:15–23	God guided Israel's journey, leading them with a pillar of cloud by day and a pillar of fire by night.
Cloud and Storm at Mount Sinai Ex. 19:16–24	God descended upon Mount Sinai in such a way that the people saw, heard, and felt his awesome presence. The mountain trembled, there was the sound of a horn, and there was thunder and lightning as a heavy cloud came down with fire.
Moses Sees God's "Back" Ex. 33:12–23	Moses asked to see God's glory, something that had been kept from him for his own sake. God allowed Moses to see his "back," thereby protecting Moses from death.
Tabernacle Ex. 25:8–9; 40:34–38; Num. 9:15–23	The tabernacle was a movable sanctuary located at the very center of the Israelite camp. God filled this tent with a cloud and his glory. In this way, God made it visibly known that he was with his people.
Ark of the Covenant Ex. 25:10–22; 37:6; Num. 14:44–45	This golden chest was the central focus of the Most Holy Place in the tabernacle. Its lid was the mercy seat of God, the unique place where God met with his people.

LAST WISHES AND DEATH

At the end of the forty-year journey, Moses and a new generation arrived at the eastern border of the promised land in the plains of Moab. This new generation did not witness firsthand God's mighty acts of salvation in Egypt nor his revelation at Sinai. They needed to be instructed in what it meant to be God's people. Their identity, based on God's law, would protect them as they entered the land and would guide them as they became a nation. The book of Deuteronomy is a collection of Moses's sermons given there on the edge of the promised land to the generation who would enter the land.

Moses's instructions in Deuteronomy can be summarized as follows:

ABOUT GOD	God is one.	Deut. 4:1–40; 6:4
	God is faithful and merciful.	Deut. 1:8, 19–46; 7:1–26; 8:1–20; 9:1–10:11
	God is powerful.	Deut. 2:1–3:11; 4:1–40; 7:1–26
ABOUT ISRAEL	God chose Israel.	Deut. 4:5–9; 10:14–15; 14:1–2, 21
	The land God promised to Israel is good.	Deut. 1:25; 6:10–11; 8:7–13; 11:8–15
	Israel must love, serve, fear, and obey God.	Deut. 6:5; 10:12–13; 13:4
	Israel must not have other gods (idolatry); rather, Israel must serve and worship God properly.	Deut. 4:9–31; 5:6–10; 7:1–5; 8:19–20; 12:1–32; 13:1–18
	God's law is meant for all areas of life in the land.	Deut. 12:1–27:26

Joshua, the faithful spy, was chosen to succeed Moses as leader. Moses climbed Mount Nebo, where God allowed him to see the promised land. Moses did not enter the land but died there. God buried him in the valley east of the Jordan River. Moses did not die of old age, nor of sickness; rather it was God's sovereign decision.

> Moses was a hundred and twenty years old when he died, yet his eyes were not weak nor his strength gone.
>
> DEUTERONOMY 34:7

MOSES AND JESUS

Because Moses is so significant, the writer of the letter to the Hebrews uses him to highlight the even greater ministry of Jesus.

> Jesus has been found worthy of greater honor than Moses, just as the builder of a house has greater honor than the house itself. For every house is built by someone, but God is the builder of everything. "Moses was faithful as a servant in all God's house," bearing witness to what would be spoken by God in the future. But Christ is faithful as the Son over God's house.
>
> HEBREWS 3:3–6

The argument that the writer of Hebrews makes to his readers could be summed up like this: If Moses, being this important, falls short before Jesus, and you believe Moses, shouldn't you believe Jesus even more?

Moses's life illustrates the human need for a mediator, and his life points to the life of the mediator we need: Jesus Christ. Moses's life shows a God full of grace and mercy, compassion and love, yet also holy and just. His life shows us the possibilities for a full relationship with God, a relationship in which we are no longer servants but friends.

Here are some ways Moses's life points to Christ:

MOSES	CHRIST
Surrounding the birth of Moses, Pharaoh killed innocent children in Egypt (Ex. 1:22).	Surrounding the birth of Jesus, King Herod killed innocent children in Bethlehem (Matt. 2:16).
Moses had to flee his native land because of Pharaoh's persecution (Ex. 2:15).	Jesus had to flee his native land because of Herod's persecution (Matt. 2:14).
Pharaoh died and Moses returned after he was told: "All those who wanted to kill you are dead" (Ex. 4:19).	Herod died and Jesus returned after "those who were trying to take the child's life are dead" (Matt. 2:20–21).
Moses fasted forty days before he delivered God's words to the people (Ex. 34:28).	Jesus fasted forty days before he began to preach (Matt. 4:2, 17).
Moses was on a mountain for the blessing of the commandments (Ex. 19:20).	Jesus was on a mount when he gave his Beatitudes and commandments (Matt. 5:1–12).
Moses's own people questioned his authority (Ex. 2:14).	Jesus's own people questioned his authority (Matt. 13:54–55).
The parting of the sea took place under Moses's command (Ex. 14:15–22).	Jesus walked on the sea and calmed the storm (Matt. 14:22–32).
A cloud overshadowed Moses, Aaron, and Miriam, and the voice of God was heard (Num. 12:5–8).	A cloud overshadowed Peter, James, and John with Jesus, and the voice of God was heard (Matt. 17:1–5).
Moses's face shown with God's glory (Ex. 34:30).	Jesus face shown with God's glory (Matt. 17:2).
God promised to raise up a prophet like Moses (Deut. 18:15).	Jesus Christ is the prophet that God promised; yet he is even greater than Moses (Heb. 3:1–6).
Moses brought God's people to the border of the promised land (Num. 33:1–56; Deut. 1:5).	Jesus brings God's people into paradise (Luke 23:43).

CHAPTER 2

Exodus Timeline and Maps

E xactly when and where the exodus occurred remains a topic of considerable debate.

Though the Bible provides a fairly detailed list of the Israelites' movements from Egypt to Sinai (Ex. 12:37–19:2; Num. 33:1–15), many of the locations are uninhabited sites and identifying them in both the ancient and modern context can be very difficult, if not impossible.

Yet we are not totally in the dark. Clues in Scripture and archaeological discoveries can narrow down the list of possibilities and shed

Amarna Letter, Egypt, c. 1353 BC

some light on when and where the exodus and the wilderness wanderings occurred. We will examine the most likely options in this chapter.

WHEN WAS THE EXODUS?

There are two main options for the date of the exodus, known as the "high date" (1446 BC) and the "low date" (1290 BC).

Evidence for the High Date (1446 BC)

✠ First Kings 6:1 states that the exodus happened four hundred and eighty years before Solomon's fourth year (around 966 BC). Working backward, this dates the exodus at 1446 BC.

✠ In Judges 11:26, Jephthah (around 1100 BC) claimed that Israel had been in Canaan for three hundred years. Adding forty years for the wilderness journey, this places the exodus around 1440 BC.

✠ The Amarna Letters/Tablets (around 1400 BC) are correspondence written between Egyptian officials and representatives in Canaan. These letters speak of a period of chaos in Canaan, which could be Joshua's conquest forty years after the exodus. The letters also make mention of a group referred to in Akkadian as the *hapiru*—social outcasts/nomads, slaves, or migrant workers—possibly the Israelites at that time.

✠ The Merneptah Stele (around 1220 BC) is an inscription recounting an Egyptian ruler's victories. The stele makes mention of "Israel" as an established group in Canaan. The low date of 1290 BC does not provide enough time for Israel to be well established by the date of this stele.

✠ The Dream Stele (1401 BC) indicates that Thutmose IV was not the firstborn legal heir to the throne, hinting at the idea that the firstborn son of Amenhotep II (1453–1426 BC) had died.

Evidence for the Low Date (1290 BC)

Merneptah Stele

✠ No references to "Israel" as a people have been discovered outside the Bible prior to the Merneptah Stele.

✠ The cities that the Bible says the Hebrews built while in Egypt (Pithom and Rameses; Ex. 1:11) were completed by Ramses II (1304–1237 BC).

✠ Biblical dating can be understood as symbolic, so the four hundred and eighty years mentioned in 1 Kings 6:1 is a period of twelve generations (forty years per generation). Biblical dates may also be exaggerated or generalized, such as Jephthah's claim of three hundred years (Judg. 11:26).

✠ The time frames for the various judges mentioned in the book of Judges may have overlapped. This would account for a shorter period of time for Joshua's conquest, settlement, and the era of judges, making the low date for the exodus possible.

As new archaeological discoveries are made, our understanding of this time period continues to grow. While there is not enough evidence to say for certain that the high date of the exodus is correct, both tradition and current research support this position more favorably than the low date. (The timeline presented in this book follows the traditional high date.)

TIMELINE OF THE EXODUS

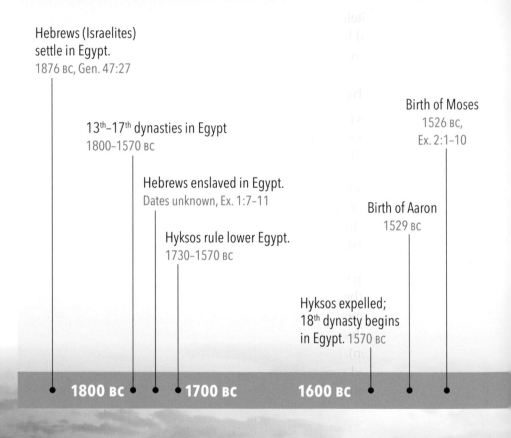

Hebrews (Israelites)
settle in Egypt.
1876 BC, Gen. 47:27

13th–17th dynasties in Egypt
1800–1570 BC

Hebrews enslaved in Egypt.
Dates unknown, Ex. 1:7–11

Hyksos rule lower Egypt.
1730–1570 BC

Hyksos expelled;
18th dynasty begins
in Egypt. 1570 BC

Birth of Moses
1526 BC,
Ex. 2:1–10

Birth of Aaron
1529 BC

1800 BC   **1700 BC**   **1600 BC**

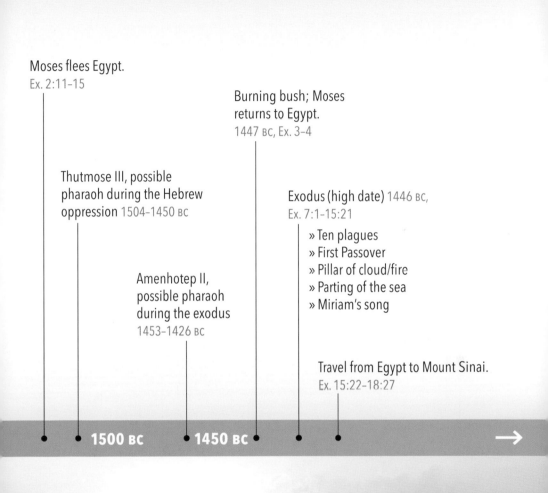

Moses flees Egypt.
Ex. 2:11–15

Thutmose III, possible
pharaoh during the Hebrew
oppression 1504–1450 BC

Burning bush; Moses
returns to Egypt.
1447 BC, Ex. 3–4

Exodus (high date) 1446 BC,
Ex. 7:1–15:21

» Ten plagues
» First Passover
» Pillar of cloud/fire
» Parting of the sea
» Miriam's song

Amenhotep II,
possible pharaoh
during the exodus
1453–1426 BC

Travel from Egypt to Mount Sinai.
Ex. 15:22–18:27

1500 BC   **1450 BC**   →

35

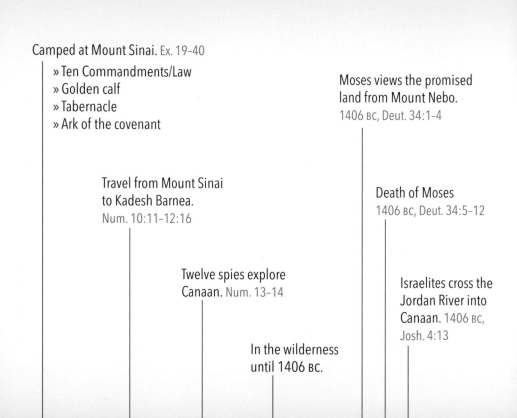

Camped at Mount Sinai. Ex. 19–40
» Ten Commandments/Law
» Golden calf
» Tabernacle
» Ark of the covenant

Travel from Mount Sinai
to Kadesh Barnea.
Num. 10:11–12:16

Twelve spies explore
Canaan. Num. 13–14

In the wilderness
until 1406 BC.

Moses views the promised
land from Mount Nebo.
1406 BC, Deut. 34:1-4

Death of Moses
1406 BC, Deut. 34:5–12

Israelites cross the
Jordan River into
Canaan. 1406 BC,
Josh. 4:13

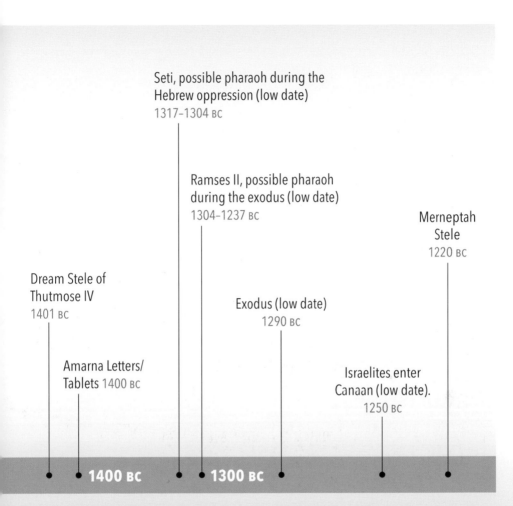

Seti, possible pharaoh during the Hebrew oppression (low date)
1317–1304 BC

Ramses II, possible pharaoh during the exodus (low date)
1304–1237 BC

Merneptah Stele
1220 BC

Dream Stele of Thutmose IV
1401 BC

Exodus (low date)
1290 BC

Amarna Letters/ Tablets 1400 BC

Israelites enter Canaan (low date).
1250 BC

1400 BC   **1300 BC**

Timeline dates are approximate. For a low date, events following the exodus (Passover, Sinai, etc.) would fall between 1290 BC and 1250 BC.

WHAT WAS THE ROUTE OF THE EXODUS?

Bible scholars have done their best to piece together the information found in Scripture along with archaeological sites and have proposed three main options for the route of the exodus.

➤ Southern Route

In this view, the Israelites would have left Goshen and headed south through the Sinai Peninsula. Traditionally, Mount Sinai is located near the southern tip of the peninsula at Jebel Musa, though some suggest it may lie a little farther north, near the Desert of Sin at Jebel Serbal.

➤ Central Route

Following this route, the Israelites took a more central path across the middle of the Sinai Peninsula. Mount Sinai may be located in Arabia/Midian at Jabal al-Lawz east of the Sinai Peninsula or at Jebel Sin Bisher in Sinai. Potential problems with this view include the harshness of the route (lack of water) and the amount of time it would take to reach the crossing point into Arabia.

➤ Northern Route

According to this view, the Israelites headed north, with Mount Sinai in the northwestern area of the Sinai Peninsula at Jebel-Helal. However, this view does not take into account that Scripture says God led Israel away from the Philistines located along the Mediterranean coast (Ex. 13:17–18). It is also inconsistent with the eleven-day journey mentioned in Deuteronomy 1:2.

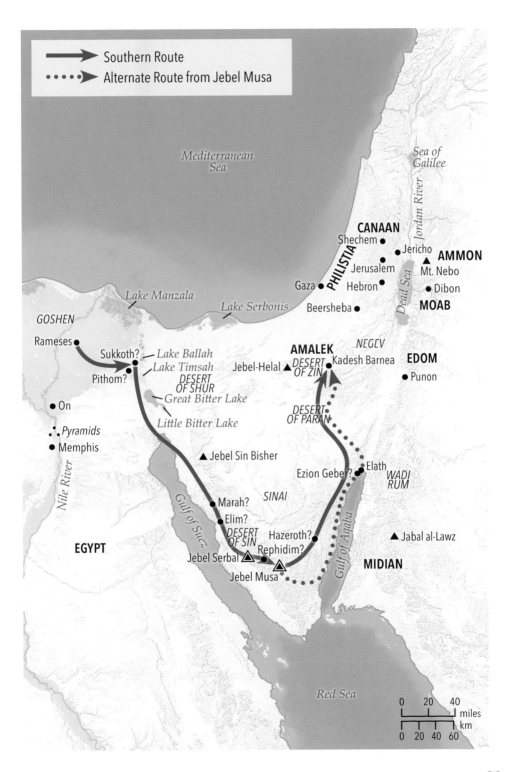

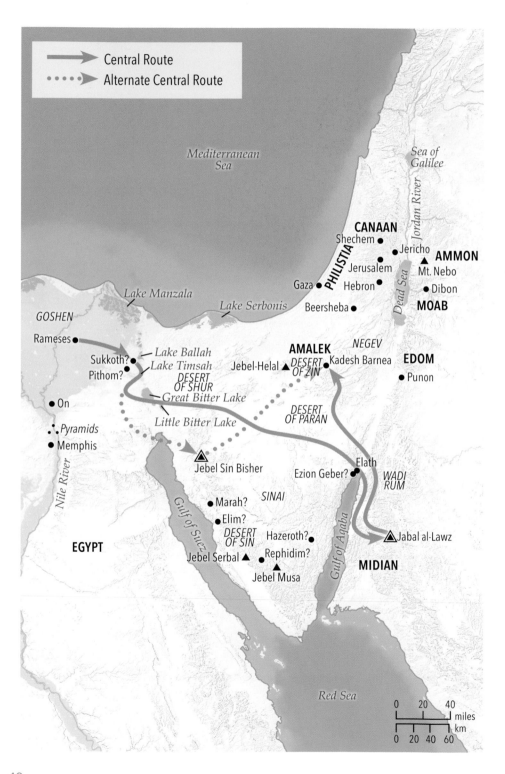

Central Route

Alternate Central Route

Mediterranean Sea

Sea of Galilee

Jordan River

CANAAN

Shechem

Jericho

AMMON

PHILISTIA

Jerusalem

Mt. Nebo

Gaza

Hebron

Dead Sea

Dibon

Beersheba

MOAB

Lake Manzala

Lake Serbonis

GOSHEN

Rameses

NEGEV

AMALEK

EDOM

Sukkoth?

Lake Ballah

Lake Timsah

Jebel-Helal

DESERT OF ZIN

Kadesh Barnea

Pithom?

DESERT OF SHUR

Punon

On

Great Bitter Lake

DESERT OF PARAN

Pyramids

Little Bitter Lake

Memphis

Nile River

Jebel Sin Bisher

Elath

Ezion Geber?

WADI RUM

SINAI

Marah?

Gulf of Suez

Elim?

Hazeroth?

Jabal al-Lawz

EGYPT

DESERT OF SIN

Rephidim?

Gulf of Aqaba

MIDIAN

Jebel Serbal

Jebel Musa

Red Sea

0	20	40
miles

km

| 0 | 20 | 40 | 60 |

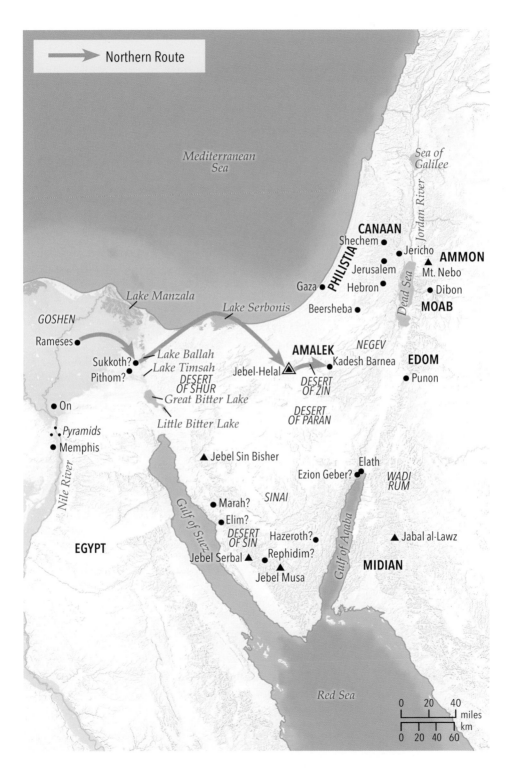

WHERE WAS THE RED SEA?

Traditionally, the Israelites are said to have crossed the "Red Sea" as they fled from Egypt (Ex. 13:18). This is based on the Greek translation of the Hebrew phrase *yam suph*. But is this what the Hebrew really says? The Hebrew word *yam* can be used for any large body of water like a sea or even a lake. *Suph* in Hebrew is actually the word for "reed," not "red." This same term is used to describe where Moses's basket was placed in the Nile River (Ex. 2:3, 5). Based on the Old Testament's use of this word, a more accurate translation for *yam suph* is "reed sea" or "sea of reeds."

The more pressing question is where was this sea located? The traditional southern route puts the sea at the tip of the Red Sea (Gulf of Suez). Also, the detailed list of places the Israelites camped says that after crossing the *yam suph* they stayed at Marah, then Elim, and then they camped by the *yam suph* again (Num. 33:8–10). If they camped next to the same body of water again, it would have to be a very large body of water, not a small lake.

Other suggested locations for the *yam suph* include Lake Ballah, Lake Timsah, Great Bitter Lake, and Little Bitter Lake. Due to the construction of the Suez Canal between the Gulf of Suez and the Mediterranean Sea, much of that area has changed, making it difficult to determine ancient water locations today.

WILDERNESS WANDERINGS

When the Israelite spies returned from Canaan with a report of good land inhabited by powerful nations, the people of Israel confined themselves to the wilderness of Sinai. For nearly forty years, they lived a semi-nomadic lifestyle, traveling wherever they could find grazing lands and water for their animals, but they stayed mostly in the region of Kadesh Barnea.

When the generation that balked at entering the promised land passed away, a new generation made its way to the edge of Canaan. Skirting enemy nations like Moab and Edom, they ended up on the plains east of the Jordan River. There, Moses delivered a last charge to the people and appointed Joshua to succeed him. Before his death, Moses climbed Mount Nebo and viewed the promised land.

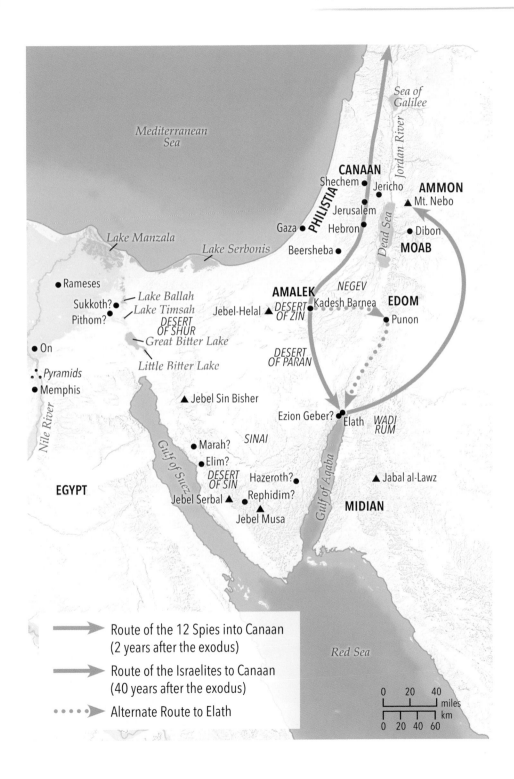

CHAPTER 3

Books of Exodus through Deuteronomy

The books of Exodus, Leviticus, Numbers, and Deuteronomy, along with the first book of the Bible, Genesis, comprise a section of the Old Testament known as the Pentateuch. The word *Pentateuch* comes from a Greek word that indicates "five vessels" or "five scrolls." These books are also known as the Law, the Torah ("instruction"), and the Books of Moses. Though often called "the Law," they are not limited to legal matters. They include narratives about the patriarchs, genealogies, sermons, songs, and stories of triumph and tragedy.

On one level, the Pentateuch is simply a collection of ancient books. But on a deeper level, the Pentateuch is God's gracious provision for the lives of his people. These five books help them answer the questions: What does it mean to be the God's people? How can a sinful people relate to a holy God? How does God relate to them? The Pentateuch is God's instructions for a nation learning to be holy people while living in an unholy world.

The Pentateuch lays the basis for the rest of the Bible. It explains the origin of the universe, of the nations, and of God's people. It explains the need for God's direct intervention in human history: human sin. The stories these books narrate show how God acts in the lives of his people.

1	**GENESIS**	**Beginnings**	50 chapters
2	**EXODUS**	**Deliverance**	40 chapters
3	**LEVITICUS**	**Holiness**	27 chapters
4	**NUMBERS**	**Wanderings**	36 chapters
5	**DEUTERONOMY**	**Instructions**	34 chapters

WHO WROTE THE PENTATEUCH?

Some Bible scholars say that Moses wrote the whole of the Pentateuch, and they offer good arguments in favor of Mosaic authorship. Others, however, argue that the collection of books underwent a long writing process which ended centuries after Moses's life. Still others will grant that Moses wrote a portion of the material, but how much is still up for debate.

There are two main arguments for recognizing Moses as the author:

1. We know from the books themselves that on several occasions God ordered Moses to write (Ex. 17:14; 24:3, 4, 7; 34:27; Lev. 26:46; 27:34; Deut. 31:9, 24).

2. Both the Old and New Testaments recognize the Pentateuch as "Moses's Law" (Josh. 8:31, 32; 1 Kings 2:3; Ezra 6:18; Neh. 8:1; Jer. 7:22; Mal. 4:4; Matt. 22:24; Acts 15:21).

However, even scholars who argue for Mosaic authorship still recognize that Moses did not write *everything* in the Pentateuch:

✠ Moses did not write about his own death (Deut. 34).

✠ Other passages that use names for cities that do not fit the times or that talk about Moses's humility were probably written by a later author (Gen. 11:31; 14:14; Num. 12:3).

✠ The text itself names ancient sources that were used in the books of the Pentateuch: the Book of the Wars of the Lord and the Book of the Covenant (Num. 21:14; Ex. 24:7). (Some scholars believe there may be other ancient sources beyond these two.)

Despite exactly how or when we think the collection of books was written, the Pentateuch remains the Word of God and lays the theological groundwork for what we read about in the rest of the Bible.

This chapter looks at the four later books of the Pentateuch—Exodus through Deuteronomy—and provides a basic summary, structure, and key verses for each book.

THE PENTATEUCH IN BIBLICAL HISTORY

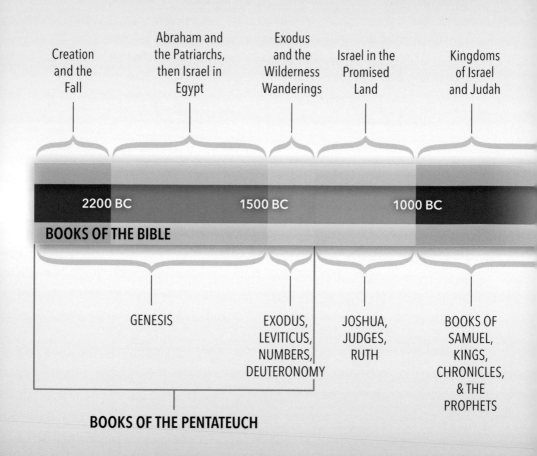

Creation and the Fall

Abraham and the Patriarchs, then Israel in Egypt

Exodus and the Wilderness Wanderings

Israel in the Promised Land

Kingdoms of Israel and Judah

2200 BC   1500 BC   1000 BC

BOOKS OF THE BIBLE

GENESIS

EXODUS, LEVITICUS, NUMBERS, DEUTERONOMY

JOSHUA, JUDGES, RUTH

BOOKS OF SAMUEL, KINGS, CHRONICLES, & THE PROPHETS

BOOKS OF THE PENTATEUCH

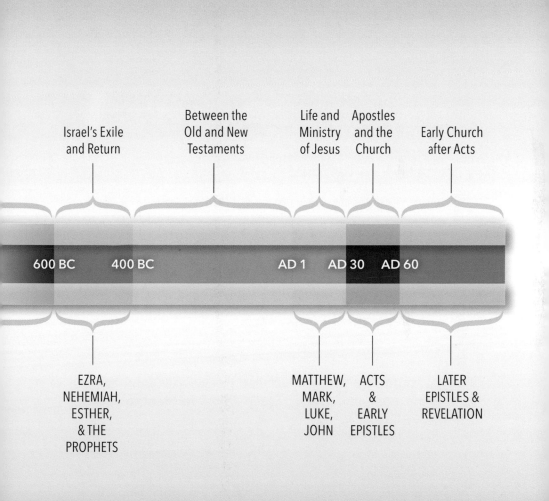

Israel's Exile
and Return

Between the
Old and New
Testaments

Life and
Ministry
of Jesus

Apostles
and the
Church

Early Church
after Acts

600 BC   400 BC   AD 1   AD 30   AD 60

EZRA,
NEHEMIAH,
ESTHER,
& THE
PROPHETS

MATTHEW,
MARK,
LUKE,
JOHN

ACTS
&
EARLY
EPISTLES

LATER
EPISTLES &
REVELATION

 # EXODUS

Summary of Exodus

The book of Exodus (which means "going out") begins several hundred years after Joseph's story which concludes the book of Genesis. Exodus tells the story of how God, through Moses, led the descendants of Jacob (Israel) out of slavery in Egypt to Mount Sinai where God gave Moses the law and made a covenant with Israel. The book closes with the Israelites at Mount Sinai where God's glory fills the newly built tabernacle.

Key Verses from Exodus

I AM WHO I AM. This is what you are to say to the Israelites: "I AM has sent me to you."

EXODUS 3:14

Go to Pharaoh and say to him, 'This is what the LORD says: Let my people go, so that they may worship me.

EXODUS 8:1

In your unfailing love you will lead the people you have redeemed. In your strength you will guide them to your holy dwelling.

EXODUS 15:13

I am the LORD your God, who brought you out of Egypt, out of the land of slavery. You shall have no other gods before me.

EXODUS 20:2–3

Outline of Exodus

1. **Israel in Egypt: God frees his people (1:1–15:21).**

   a. Israelites are enslaved in Egypt (1:1–2:25).

   b. God calls Moses through a burning bush (3:1–4:31).

   c. God sends ten plagues upon Egypt and the first Passover is observed (5:1–12:30).

   d. Israelites leave Egypt and God parts the sea (12:31–15:21).

2. **Israel on the way toward Sinai: God travels with his people (15:22–18:27).**

   a. God provides manna and quail (15:22–16:36).

   b. God provides water from a rock (17:1–7).

   c. Israelites defeat the Amalekites (17:8–16).

   d. Moses appoints leaders (18:1–27).

3. **Israel at Sinai: God instructs and organizes his people (19:1–40:38).**

   a. Moses meets with God on Mount Sinai (19:1–25).

   b. God gives the Ten Commandments (20:1–17).

   c. God gives laws for Israel and instructions for the tabernacle (20:18–31:18).

   d. The people worship the golden calf (32:1–32:29).

   e. Moses meets with God again (32:30–35:3).

   f. Moses and the people build the tabernacle (35:4–40:38).

COVENANTS IN THE BIBLE

Adamic Covenant

Gen. 1:26–30; 2:15–17

Who: God, Adam and Eve, all creation
When: At creation
What: Provision for all God's creation

Noahic Covenant

Gen. 8:20–9:17

Who: God, Noah, every living creature
When: After the flood
What: Never again destroy the world in a flood

Abrahamic Covenant

Gen. 12:1–7

Who: God, Abraham
When: Abraham at age 75; 2091 BC
What: Descendants and the promised land

Mosaic Covenant

Ex. 19:3–8

Who: God, Moses, Israel
When: After the exodus; 1446 BC (or 1290 BC)
What: Blessings if Israel obeys God's law

Davidic Covenant

2 Sam. 7:4–17

Who: God, King David
When: David's reign; 1000 BC
What: Establish David's throne forever

New Covenant

Jer. 31:31–34; Matt. 26:28; Heb. 8:6

Who: God, Jesus, all who trust in Jesus
When: Jesus' death and resurrection; AD 30
What: New relationship, eternal life, superior covenant

LEVITICUS

Summary of Leviticus

The book of Leviticus takes place within the two years that the Israelites spent camped at the foot of Mount Sinai. Leviticus is a series of divine directives about sacrifices, priestly duties, ritual purity, feasts of Israel, and holy ("set apart") living. Though the book's name comes from the Greek word *leyiticon* that means "things concerning the Levites," the book was not only for the tribe of Levi, but rather includes instructions for the entire nation of Israel.

Key Verses from Leviticus

Be holy, because I am holy.

LEVITICUS 11:45

For the life of a creature is in the blood, and I have given it to you to make atonement for yourselves on the altar; it is the blood that makes atonement for one's life.

LEVITICUS 17:11

Do not seek revenge or bear a grudge against anyone among your people, but love your neighbor as yourself.

LEVITICUS 19:18

I will put my dwelling place [tabernacle] among you, and I will not abhor you. I will walk among you and be your God, and you will be my people.

LEVITICUS 26:11–12

Outline of Leviticus

1. **Instructions for offerings (1:1–7:38)**

   a. Burnt offering (1:1–17)

   b. Grain offering (2:1–16)

   c. Fellowship offering (3:1–17)

   d. Sin offering (4:1–13)

   e. Guilt offering (4:14–6:7)

   f. More instructions for offerings (6:8–7:38)

2. **Instructions for priests (8:1–10:20)**

   a. Aaron and his sons (8:1–36)

   b. The priests present offerings (9:1–10:20)

3. **Instructions for purity (11:1–15:33)**

   a. Clean and unclean foods (11:1–47)

   b. Impurities and cleansing rituals (12:1–15:33)

4. **Instructions for the Day of Atonement (16:1–34)**

5. **Instructions for holy living (17:1–27:34)**

   a. Animal sacrifices (17:1–16)

   b. Sexual relations (18:1–30)

   c. Punishment for sins (19:1–20:27)

   d. Priestly requirements (21:1–22:33)

   e. Sabbath, feasts, and the Year of Jubilee (23:1–25:55)

   f. God's favor and the consequences of disobedience (26:1–27:34)

HOLY LIVING

Sacrifices

Sacrifices (or offerings) were God's merciful provision for Israel so the people could dwell with a holy God. In the Old Testament, the shedding and use of animal blood for the purifying and atoning rituals was a reminder for the worshiper of the high penalty for sin. The sacrifices made atonement and thus allowed the Israelites to dwell alongside God as his presence dwelt in the tabernacle in their camp.

Sacrifices today are not necessary because Jesus's sacrifice on the cross was the perfect and sufficient atonement for sin. Yet our need to accept that gift of atonement through faith remains.

The Priesthood

Priests were intermediaries. At different moments and in different ways during their ministries, priests stood in the gap that separates God and humans. Their holiness did not come from their actions or position. Rather, their holiness depended on their nearness to the tabernacle—to God's presence. As representatives of the people, the priests were held to rigorous moral, ritual, and purity standards.

In the New Testament, the apostle Paul explains that now there is only "one mediator between God and mankind, the man Christ Jesus" (1 Tim. 2:5).

Purity

Purity was necessary as people lived around the tabernacle. God's presence rejected the ritually impure. Purification rites were God's provision for the people to be able to approach his presence.

Today, the blood that Christ shed on the cross purifies us and makes us fit to approach God's presence. Instead of ritual purity, today we are called to live in godly ways that reflect the goodness and love of God (2 Peter 1:3–8).

NUMBERS

Summary of Numbers

The book of Numbers narrates the years of wilderness wanderings after the Israelites left Mount Sinai. The book is named Numbers because of the two censuses recorded in chapters 1 and 26. In Exodus, God had promised the Israelites that he would be with them on their way out of captivity. In Numbers, we see God remaining faithful to this promise despite his people's unfaithfulness and rebellion. The book ends with the Israelites camped in the plains of Moab just outside the promised land.

Key Verses from Numbers

The LORD is slow to anger, abounding in love and forgiving sin and rebellion. Yet he does not leave the guilty unpunished.

NUMBERS 14:18

The LORD bless you and keep you; the LORD make his face shine on you and be gracious to you; the LORD turn his face toward you and give you peace.

NUMBERS 6:24–26

God is not human, that he should lie, not a human being, that he should change his mind. Does he speak and then not act? Does he promise and not fulfill?

NUMBERS 23:19

Outline of Numbers

1. **The end of the first generation (1:1–25:18)**

   a. First census is taken (1:1–4:49).

   b. Regulations for purity and offerings (5:1–10:10).

   c. Israelites leave Sinai and grumble (10:11–12:16).

   d. Twelve spies explore Canaan and the people rebel (13:1–16:50).

   e. God instructs Moses and Aaron (17:1–19:22).

   f. Israelites face challenges: thirst, venomous snakes, hostile nations (20:1–25:18).

2. **The birth of the new generation (26:1–36:13)**

   a. Second census is taken (26:1–65).

   b. Inheritance laws are given for the new generation (27:1–11).

   c. Joshua is commissioned to succeed Moses (27:12–23).

   d. Laws given for offerings, feasts, and vows (28:1–30:16).

   e. Israelites defeat their enemies (31:1–32:42).

   f. Moses gives instructions to the next generation (33:1–36:13).

THE WILDERNESS

In the book of Numbers, the wilderness becomes a key part of the story. In addition to the literal meaning of the wilderness (the Israelites had to cross the desert to get to the promised land), the concept of the wilderness has a symbolic meaning. It represented a place of danger, of death and barrenness, of chaos and darkness. It is seen as a life-negating reality that opposes God's life-giving will (Num. 14:35).

However, the wilderness also came to represent a place of transition, a place for meeting God. The tabernacle, the visual representation of God's dwelling, became a place of life, hope, order, and light for Israel.

Both generations of Israelites got to witness God provide for their needs with amazing miracles and victories against all odds.

THE CENSUSES

The census numbers report a fighting force of about 600,000, which would suggest a general population of over two million. Such a large population wandering in the desert for forty years would require a miracle to be supported—and that is precisely what happened. God sustained his people through their decades-long journey.

TRIBE	FIRST CENSUS	SECOND CENSUS
REUBEN	46,500	43,730
SIMEON	59,300	22,200
LEVI*	22,000	23,000
JUDAH	74,600	76,500
DAN	62,700	64,400
NAPHTALI	53,400	45,400
GAD	45,650	40,500
ASHER	41,500	53,400
ISSACHAR	54,400	64,300
ZEBULUN	57,400	60,500
MANASSEH	32,200	52,700
EPHRAIM	40,500	32,500
BENJAMIN	35,400	45,600

*Not counted as fighting men, but caretakers of the tabernacle.

DEUTERONOMY

Summary of Deuteronomy

The entire book of Deuteronomy takes place while Israel is camped at the border of the promised land, east of the Jordan River in the plains of Moab.

The book's name comes from the Greek word *deuteronomion* meaning "second law." Deuteronomy consists of encouraging and challenging speeches (or sermons) Moses gave to the next generation as they were about to enter Canaan. They are challenged to remember and learn from the mistakes of the previous generation.

To the east of the Jordan River, the majestic Mount Nebo was a silent witness of Israel's preparations to enter the land. On Mount Nebo, Moses saw the promised land. The book of Deuteronomy (and the Pentateuch) closes with Moses's death.

Key Verses from Deuteronomy

Hear, O Israel: The LORD our God, the LORD is one. Love the LORD your God with all your heart and with all your soul and with all your strength.

DEUTERONOMY 6:4–5

The LORD your God will raise up for you a prophet like me from among you, from your fellow Israelites. You must listen to him.

DEUTERONOMY 18:15

This day I call the heavens and the earth as witnesses against you that I have set before you life and death, blessings and curses. Now choose life, so that you and your children may live.

DEUTERONOMY 30:19

Outline of Deuteronomy

1. **A look backward (1:1–3:29)**

   a. Moses summarizes the wilderness journey (1:1–3:20).

   b. Moses summarizes Joshua's commission (3:21–29).

2. **The great discourse (4:1–11:32)**

   a. Moses tells the people to remember and obey God's decrees (4:1–49).

   b. Moses lists the Ten Commandments (5:1–33).

   c. Moses tells the people to love and fear God (6:1–11:32).

3. **Covenant stipulations (12:1–26:19)**

   a. Moses tells the people to worship the one true God (12:1–13:18).

   b. Moses gives various laws for Israel (14:1–26:19).

4. **Covenant ceremony (27:1–30:20)**

5. **A look forward (31:1–34:12)**

   a. Joshua confirmed as Moses's successor (31:1–29).

   b. The song of Moses (31:30–32:52).

   c. Moses blesses the tribes (33:1–29).

   d. Moses dies on Mount Nebo (34:1–12).

A Covenantal Outline

Some Bible scholars believe Deuteronomy was written according to the structure of ancient covenant documents. In this understanding, the book of Deuteronomy could be outlined like this: Preamble (1:1–5), Historical Prologue (1:6–4:43), Stipulations of the Covenant (4:44–26:19), Ratification: Curses and Blessings (27–30), Leadership Succession under the Covenant (31–34).

EXODUS THROUGH DEUTERONOMY IN THE GOSPELS

NEW TESTAMENT	OLD TESTAMENT
Joseph and Mary took the infant Jesus to the temple in Jerusalem to be dedicated, and they offered a sacrifice of two birds according to the law (Luke 2:22–24).	"Consecrate to me every firstborn male" (Ex. 13:2). "Bring two doves or two young pigeons, one for a burnt offering and the other for a sin offering" (Lev. 12:8).
Joseph, Mary, and the child Jesus left Egypt where they had fled from King Herod (Matt. 2:14–15).	Matthew quotes the prophecy in Hosea recalling the exodus: "Out of Egypt I called my son" (Hos. 11:1; Ex. 4:22).
As a child, Jesus and his family observed Passover every year in Jerusalem (Luke 2:41–42).	Passover was observed by all Israel, annually in the first month of the year (Deut. 16:16; Lev. 23:4–8).
When tempted by Satan to turn stones into bread, Jesus replied with scripture from Deuteronomy: "Man shall not live on bread alone, but on every word that comes from the mouth of God" (Matt. 4:4).	Moses said this to the Israelites to explain that God allowed them to face hunger in the wilderness so they would learn to rely on the word of the Lord (Deut. 8:3).
When Satan told Jesus to prove he was the Son of God, Jesus again replied with Scripture: "It is also written: 'Do not put the Lord your God to the test'" (Matt. 4:7).	With these words, Moses warned the Israelites not to test the Lord (Deut. 6:16; Ex. 17:2).
When Satan offered Jesus the world if Jesus would worship him, Jesus quoted Deuteronomy: "Worship the Lord your God, and serve him only" (Matt. 4:10).	Before the Israelites entered the promised land, Moses urged them to "fear the LORD your God [and] serve him only" (Deut. 6:13).

NEW TESTAMENT	OLD TESTAMENT
After meeting Jesus, Philip recognized him as "the one Moses wrote about in the Law" (John 1:45).	"The LORD your God will raise up for you a prophet like me from among you, from your fellow Israelites. You must listen to him" (Deut. 18:15; see also Acts 3:22).
Jesus explained, "Just as Moses lifted up the snake in the wilderness, so the Son of Man must be lifted up, that everyone who believes may have eternal life in him" (John 3:14–15).	Moses made a bronze snake and put it on a pole, and if anyone was bitten, they could look at the bronze snake and be healed (Num. 21:4–9).
Jesus said that Moses's writings speak of him, and he referred to the first five books of the Hebrew Bible as "the Book of Moses" (John 5:46–47; Mark 12:26).	"Moses wrote down this law and gave it … to all the elders of Israel" (Deut. 31:9).
Jesus cited the fifth commandment as one the religious leaders set aside in favor of their own traditions (Matt. 15:4; Mark 7:10).	"Honor your father and your mother" (Ex. 20:12; Deut. 5:16).
Jesus extended the sixth commandment beyond actions to matters of the heart (Matt. 5:21–22).	"You shall not murder" (Ex. 20:13; Deut. 5:17).
Jesus extended the seventh commandment to show that thoughts make one just as guilty (Matt. 5:27–28).	"You shall not commit adultery" (Ex. 20:14; Deut. 5:18).
In his discussion with the rich young ruler, Jesus cited from the Ten Commandments and a teaching in Leviticus (Matt. 19:18–19; Mark 10:19; Luke 18:20).	Honor your parents. You shall not murder, commit adultery, steal, or give false testimony (Ex. 20:12–16). "Love your neighbor as yourself" (Lev. 19:18).

NEW TESTAMENT	OLD TESTAMENT
Jesus said, "You have heard that it was said to the people long ago, 'Do not break your oath, but fulfill to the Lord the vows you have made'" (Matt. 5:33).	"When a man makes a vow to the Lord or takes an oath to obligate himself by a pledge, he must not break his word but must do everything he said" (Num. 30:2).
Jesus challenged common interpretations of Old Testament laws, such as "eye for eye, and tooth for tooth" (Matt. 5:38).	This law was intended to make the punishment fit the crime, not give permission for revenge (Ex. 21:23–25; Lev. 24:20; Deut. 19:21).
Jesus said, "Be merciful, just as your Father is merciful" (Luke 6:36).	"The compassionate and gracious God … forgiving wickedness, rebellion and sin" (Ex. 34:6–7; also Lev. 11:45).
Jesus compared the temporary manna that ancient Israel ate with the eternal bread of life (John 6:58).	God provided manna in the wilderness as food for his people (Ex. 16:1–35).
Jesus applied the divine name to himself, leaving no doubt of his claim to be God: "Before Abraham was born, I am" (John 8:58).	God said to Moses, "I AM WHO I AM. This is what you are to say to the Israelites: 'I AM has sent me to you'" (Ex. 3:14).
At Jesus's transfiguration, Moses and Elijah appeared (Matt. 17:1–3).	Moses was arguably the greatest prophet of the Old Testament (Deut. 34:10).
Observing the people's lack of faith, Jesus remarked, "You unbelieving and perverse generation" (Matt. 17:17; Mark 9:19; Luke 9:41).	"They are a perverse generation" (Deut. 32:30).
Jesus used a law in Deuteronomy to establish his divine authority and also to teach about restoring a fallen believer (Matt. 18:15–17; John 8:14–18).	The law of Moses required the testimony of a minimum of two witnesses (Deut. 19:15).

NEW TESTAMENT	OLD TESTAMENT
Jesus alluded to Deuteronomy to teach that devotion to God should come before even good deeds like helping the poor (Mark 14:7; John 12:8).	"There will always be poor people in the land. Therefore I command you to be openhanded toward your fellow Israelites who are poor" (Deut. 15:11).
In defense of the resurrection, Jesus quoted from Exodus to show that God is the God of the living (Matt. 22:31–32; Mark 12:26; Luke 20:37).	"I am the God of your father, the God of Abraham, the God of Isaac and the God of Jacob" (Ex. 3:6).
Jesus prefaced his answer about the greatest commandment by affirming a central tenet of Jewish faith found in Deuteronomy (Mark 12:29).	"Hear, O Israel: The LORD our God, the LORD is one" (Deut. 6:4).
Jesus said the greatest commandment is to love God with one's whole being (Matt. 22:37–39; Mark 12:30).	"Love the LORD your God with all your heart and with all your soul and with all your strength" (Deut. 6:5).
Jesus said the second greatest commandment is to love others (Matt. 22:37–39; Mark 12:31).	"Love your neighbor as yourself" (Lev. 19:18).
At his last Passover meal, Jesus instituted a commemoration of the new covenant based on his sacrificial death (Matt. 26:2; Mark 14:14; Luke 22:8).	Passover commemorates the Israelites' deliverance from slavery in Egypt: "This is a day you are to commemorate … a lasting ordinance" (Ex. 12:14).
On the cross, none of Jesus's bones were broken (John 19:36).	None of the Passover lamb's bones were broken (Ex. 12:46).

CHAPTER 4

Who's Who in the Exodus

Aaron

EX. 4:14–16; 28:1–2; 32; LEV. 8–9;
NUM. 12; 17:6–11; 20:22–29

Aaron was Moses and Miriam's
brother. When Moses claimed to
be inadequate, God commissioned
Aaron to speak for Moses. Aaron
accompanied Moses to Pharaoh's
court to demand the Israelites'
release. In the wilderness, God
appointed Aaron as the first
high priest of Israel and decreed
all high priests must be Aaron's
descendants. Despite this, Aaron
gave in to the Israelites' demands
for an idol and created the golden

Aaron turning the Nile waters to blood

calf. Aaron did not arrive at the promised land. He died on Mount Hor at
123 years old. The Israelites mourned him for thirty days.

Abihu

EX. 6:23; 28:1, 40–43; 29; LEV. 10:1–2; NUM. 3:4

Abihu was Aaron's second son who was consecrated as a priest of Israel
alongside his father and brothers. Abihu and his brother Nadab offered
"unauthorized fire" before the Lord at the tabernacle's altar against God's
command. For this infraction, they were consumed by holy fire from the
Lord and died.

Abiram

See *Korah, Dathan, and Abiram*.

Asher (Tribe)

NUM. 1:40–41; 2:27–28; 26:44–47; DEUT. 33:24–25

This tribe was descended from Jacob's son Asher. The tribe's population
significantly increased between the two censuses. Moses blessed the tribe
saying, "Let him be favored by his brothers, and let him bathe his feet in
oil." Moses referred to Asher as the "most blessed" tribe.

Balaam

NUM. 22:5–39; 23–24; 31:7–16

Balaam, a pagan prophet, was asked to curse Israel by King Balak. He initially refused, but the Lord permitted him to go only if he did as the Lord commanded. Balaam followed the Lord's command and blessed Israel three times. But later, he encouraged the Moabite women to entice the Israelite men into worshiping Baal, a pagan god. The Israelites killed Balaam when the Lord ordered them to take vengeance on the Moabites.

Balak

NUM. 22:2–18, 36–40; 23–24

Balak was a Moabite king who feared the Israelites after seeing what they had done to the Amorites. The king attempted to hire Balaam to curse them and brought him to three different altars to do so. Balaam failed to curse the Israelites by God's command. In his anger, King Balak sent Balaam away and refused to pay him. The Bible does not specify what happened to the king, only that he "went his own way."

Benjamin (Tribe)

NUM. 1:36–37; 2:22–23; 26:38–41; DEUT. 33:12

This tribe was descended from Jacob's son Benjamin. The tribe's population increased between the two censuses. Moses blessed the tribe saying, "Let the beloved of the Lord rest secure in him, for he shields him all day long, and the one the Lord loves rests between his shoulders."

Bezalel

EX. 31:2–50; 35:30–35; 36:1–7; 37:1–9; 38:22–23

God chose Bezalel to be the chief designer of the tabernacle's furnishings and the sacred garments for Aaron and the priests. God filled Bezalel with the Spirit, granting him wisdom, knowledge, understanding, and skill in "all kinds of crafts."

Bezalel

Caleb

NUM. 13:3–14:38; 26:65

Caleb was a leader of the tribe of Judah sent out by Moses to explore Canaan as a spy. Caleb and Joshua were the only two spies to come back with a positive report. Swayed by the other ten's negative report, the Israelites became afraid. This angered God, and he declared the people would wander in the wilderness for forty years until the old generation (anyone twenty or older) died. Caleb and Joshua were the only members of the old generation allowed to enter the promised land.

SPIES SENT TO CANAAN (NUM. 13:1–16)

SPY	TRIBE	REPORT
SHAMMUA	RUBEN	NEGATIVE
SHAPHAT	SIMEON	NEGATIVE
CALEB	JUDAH	POSITIVE
AMMIEL	DAN	NEGATIVE
NAHBI	NAPHTALI	NEGATIVE
GEUEL	GAD	NEGATIVE
SETHUR	ASHER	NEGATIVE
IGAL	ISSACHAR	NEGATIVE
GADDIEL	ZEBULUN	NEGATIVE
GADDI	MANASSEH	NEGATIVE
HOSHEA (JOSHUA)	EPHRAIM	POSITIVE
PALTI	BENJAMIN	NEGATIVE

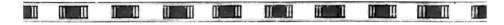

Dan (Tribe)

NUM. 1:38–39; 2:25–26, 31; 26:42–43; DEUT. 33:22

This tribe was descended from Jacob's son Dan. The tribe's population slightly increased between the two censuses. Moses blessed the tribe saying, "Dan is a lion's cub, springing out of Bashan."

Dathan

See *Korah, Dathan, and Abiram*.

Eldad and Medad

NUM. 11:26–29

Eldad and Medad were two of the seventy Israelite elders chosen by Moses to help with administration. God filled them with his Spirit, and the men began prophesying in the camp. Upset, Joshua urged Moses to stop them, but Moses refused and instead said that he wished all the Lord's people were prophets.

Eleazar

EX. 6:23; 28:1; LEV. 10:6–16; NUM. 3:2–4, 32; 20:25–29; 27:18–23; 34:16–7

Eleazar was Aaron's third son and the chief leader of the Levites. He was consecrated as a priest of Israel along with his father and brothers. After the deaths of his older brothers Nadab and Abihu, and the death of his father, Eleazar succeeded Aaron as Israel's high priest. He helped Moses conduct the second census, and later commissioned Joshua to take over Moses's position.

Eliezer

EX. 18:4

Eliezer was Moses's second son by Zipporah, whose name means "My father's God was my helper; he saved me from the sword of Pharaoh."

Elisheba

EX. 6:23

Elisheba was Aaron's wife and the mother of Nadab, Abihu, Eleazar, and Ithamar. Her brother Nahshon was a leader of Judah.

Elzaphan

See *Mishael and Elzaphan.*

Ephraim (Tribe)

NUM. 1:32–35; 2:18–21, 24; 26:28–37; DEUT. 33:13–17

This tribe was descended from Jacob's son Joseph, specifically through Joseph's son Ephraim. This tribe's population decreased between the two censuses. Moses blessed the tribes of Ephraim and Manasseh (the two tribes of Joseph) saying, "May the Lord bless his land … with the best gifts of the earth and its fullness."

Gad (Tribe)

NUM. 1:24–25; 2:14–15; 26:15–18; DEUT. 33:20–21

This tribe was descended from Jacob's son Gad. The tribe's population decreased between the two censuses. Moses praised the tribe for "carrying out the Lord's righteous will, and his judgments concerning Israel." Moses also blessed anyone who "enlarges Gad's domain."

Gershom

EX. 2:22; 18:3

Gershom was Moses's first son by Zipporah, whose name means "I have become a foreigner in a foreign land," referring to Moses's flight to Midian after killing an Egyptian.

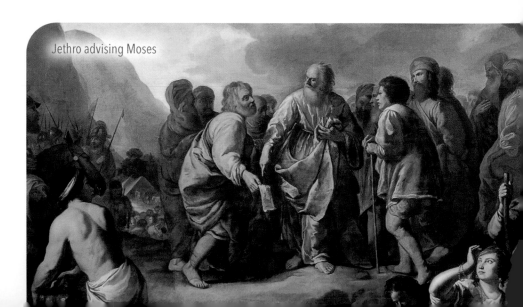

Jethro advising Moses

Hobab

NUM. 10:29–33

Hobab was Jethro's son and Moses's brother-in-law, the brother of his wife Zipporah. Moses invited Hobab to join the Israelites on their journey to the promised land. He refused, though Moses insisted. Hobab's response to this second plea is not recorded in Scripture, though it is implied he changed his mind and joined them.

Hur

EX. 17:8–13; 24:12–14

Hur assisted Aaron in holding up Moses's arms so the Israelites would win against the Amalekites. Later, Hur helped Aaron settle disputes among the people when Moses and Joshua went up to Mount Sinai.

Issachar (Tribe)

NUM. 1:28–29; 2:5–6; 26:23–25; DEUT. 33:18–19

This tribe was descended from Jacob's son Issachar. This tribe's population increased between the two censuses. Moses blessed

Hur and Aaron helping Moses

Issachar and Zebulun together saying, "They will feast on the abundance of the seas, on the treasures hidden in the sand."

Ithamar

EX. 28:1; 38:21; LEV. 10:6–16; NUM. 3:4; 4:29–33

Ithamar was Aaron's fourth and youngest son. He was consecrated as a priest of Israel alongside his father and brothers. Along with Eleazar, Ithamar was one of Aaron's two surviving sons. He was a leader for the Levites.

Jethro (Reuel)

EX. 2:18–21; 3:1; 4:18–11; 18; NUM. 10:29–33; DEUT. 11:6

Jethro, also called Reuel, was a priest in Midian and Moses's father-in-law whom Moses worked for as a shepherd. After Moses and the Israelites left

Egypt in the exodus, Jethro, Moses's wife Zipporah, and Moses's sons met Moses at Mount Sinai. When Jethro saw how busy Moses was managing the people, he advised him to appoint judges for minor disputes while still hearing the difficult cases. Moses took his advice, and Jethro returned to Midian.

Jochebed

EX. 1:22–2:10; 6:20; NUM. 26:59

Jochebed was the mother of Aaron, Moses, and Miriam. To save baby Moses from death, she placed him in a basket among the reeds along the bank of the Nile River. When Pharaoh's daughter found him, she commissioned Jochebed to nurse him. Jochebed gave Moses back to Pharaoh's daughter once he was weaned.

Joshua (Hoshea)

EX. 17:9–14; 24:13; 33:11; NUM. 13:3–14:38; 27:15–22; DEUT. 31:1–23; 34:9

Joshua (born Hoshea, name changed by Moses) was Moses's "aid since youth" (Num. 11:28) and later his successor. Joshua led the Israelites in victory against the Amalekites and joined Moses on Mount Sinai. Joshua,

Israelite spies return from Canaan

a leader of the tribe of Ephraim, was chosen as one of the twelve spies to scope out Canaan. He and Caleb were the only spies to come back with a positive report. Because they demonstrated trust in God, Joshua and Caleb were the only people from the first generation whom God said would enter the promised land. Upon Moses's death, Joshua became "filled with the spirit of wisdom" (Deut. 34:9).

Judah (Tribe)

NUM. 1:26–27; 2:3–4, 9; 10:14; 26:19–22; DEUT. 33:7

This tribe was descended from Jacob's son Judah. Moses blessed Judah, asking God to "hear … the cry of Judah; bring him to his people. With his own hands he defends his cause. Oh, be his help against his foes!" Judah was the largest tribe and the leader of the tribes as they marched through the wilderness.

Korah, Dathan, and Abiram

NUM. 16:1–35; 26:8–11; DEUT. 11:6

These three men led 250 others in an uprising against Moses. Korah, a Levite, alleged Moses and Aaron put themselves above the Lord's assembly, while brothers Dathan and Abiram from the tribe of Reuben were angry with Moses's failure to bring them to the promised land. As punishment, the

Death of Korah, Dathan and Abiram

Lord opened the earth, and it swallowed all three men and their families (though Korah's line did not completely die out). The other 250 were consumed by fire as they offered incense.

Levi (Tribe)

NUM. 1:47–53; 2:17; 3; 26:57–62; DEUT. 33:8–11

This tribe was descended from Jacob's son Levi. Moses, Miriam, and Aaron were from this tribe. God set the Levites apart, choosing them as priests, attendants, and caretakers of the tabernacle. Because they were distinguished from the rest of the Israelites, they were counted separately in the first census, and not as fighting men. Moses blessed the tribe of Levi, asking God to "be pleased with the work of his hands. Strike down those who rise against him, his foes till they rise no more."

Magicians of Pharaoh's Court

EX. 7:11–12; 7:22–24; 8:7, 18–19; 9:11

Pharaoh called upon his magicians to replicate God's miracles to discredit God, Moses, and Aaron. They could replicate the first three miracles, but not the last seven. When afflicted with boils, they were unable to stand before Moses. They told Pharaoh that the miracles were "the finger of God," but Pharaoh did not listen.

Manasseh (Tribe)

NUM. 1:32–35; 2:18–21, 24; 26:28–37; DEUT. 33:13–17

This tribe was descended from Jacob's son Joseph, specifically through Joseph's son Manasseh. This tribe's population significantly increased between the two censuses. Moses blessed the tribes of Manasseh and Ephraim (the two tribes of Joseph) saying, "May the Lord bless his land … with the best gifts of the earth and its fullness."

Medad

See *Eldad and Medad*.

Miriam

EX. 2:1–10; 15:19–21; NUM. 12; 20:1

Miriam was a prophet and the sister of Moses and Aaron. She was most likely the sister in Exodus 2 who assisted in saving baby Moses. After the exodus, Miriam led the Israelite women in song and dance when they crossed the parted sea. When Miriam and Aaron criticized Moses, Miriam was punished with leprosy. Aaron and Moses begged God to heal her. She was forced to live outside the camp for seven days, after which God healed and restored her. Miriam died before reaching the promised land and was buried at Kadesh in the wilderness.

Mishael and Elzaphan

LEV. 10:4–5

Mishael and Elzaphan were Moses and Aaron's cousins who carried the bodies of Nadab and Abihu out of the camp after their deaths.

Miriam

Moses

EX. 2–11; 13:17–19:25; 24; 32–34; NUM. 11–14; 20–21; 31; DEUT. 1:1; 31–34

Rescued as an infant and raised by Pharaoh's daughter, Moses fled Egypt after killing an Egyptian who was beating a Hebrew slave. Moses became a shepherd in Midian, but from a burning bush, God instructed him to bring his people out of Egypt. Moses guided them through the wilderness for nearly forty years. Moses's relationship with God was unique, for God met with Moses "face to face clearly and not in riddles; he [Moses] sees the form of the Lord" (Num. 12:8). Moses represented Israel to God and God to Israel. Though Moses was forbidden from entering Canaan, God allowed him a view of it before he died. Moses died in the plains of Moab at the edge of the promised land at 120 years old.

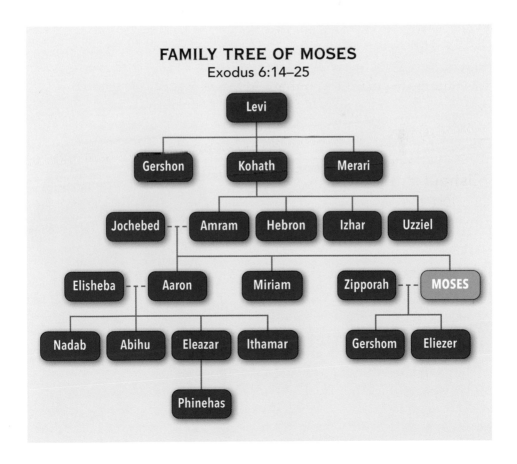

FAMILY TREE OF MOSES
Exodus 6:14–25

Levi

Gershon — Kohath — Merari

Jochebed – – Amram — Hebron — Izhar — Uzziel

Elisheba – – Aaron — Miriam — Zipporah – – MOSES

Nadab — Abihu — Eleazar — Ithamar — Gershom — Eliezer

Phinehas

Nadab

EX. 28:1, 40–43; 29; LEV. 8–9; 10:1–2; NUM. 3:4

Nadab was Aaron's first son who was consecrated as a priest of Israel alongside his father and brothers. Nadab and his brother Abihu offered "unauthorized fire" before the Lord at the tabernacle's altar against his command. For this infraction, they were consumed by holy fire from the Lord and died.

Naphtali (Tribe)

NUM. 1:42–43; 2:29–30; 26:48–50; DEUT. 33:23

This tribe was descended from Jacob's son Naphtali. This tribe's population decreased between the two censuses. Moses blessed the tribe, saying it was "abounding with favor from the Lord and is full of his blessing."

Og

NUM. 21; DEUT. 3

Og, king of Bashan, marched out with his army to meet Israel in battle. The Israelites defeated and killed Og, his sons, and the whole army in battle.

Oholiab

EX. 31:6; 35:34–35; 36:1–7; 38:22–23

God blessed Oholiab with the ability of craftsmanship. Oholiab assisted Bezalel in creating the tabernacle's furnishings.

Pharaoh

EX. 1; 4:19; 5–11; 12:29–32; 14:1–28

Pharaoh is the title used for ancient kings in Egypt. Exodus depicts two pharaohs, both unnamed in Scripture. The first pharaoh enslaved the Israelites and was the father of Moses's adopted mother. He died after Moses left Egypt. Moses and Aaron confronted the succeeding pharaoh, who, after ten terrible plagues, let the Israelites go. But when he changed his mind, his army chased them down and drowned in the sea.

Pharaoh's Daughter

EX. 2:5–10

Pharaoh's daughter (unnamed in Scripture) found baby Moses in the reeds in the Nile River and raised him as her own.

Phinehas

NUM. 25:7–13; 31:6

Phinehas was the son of Eleazar and the grandson of Aaron. While an Israelite man continued to sleep with

Pharaoh's daughter finding baby Moses

a Moabite woman, Phinehas drove a spear through them both, stopping the plague on the Israelites. Because his actions honored God, God promised Phinehas that his descendants would be priests in Israel forever.

Puah

See *Shiphrah and Puah.*

Reuel

See *Jethro.*

Reuben (Tribe)

NUM. 1:20–21; 2:10–11, 16; 26:5–6; DEUT. 33:6

This tribe was descended from Jacob's son Reuben. This tribe's population decreased between the two censuses. Moses blessed the tribe saying, "Let Reuben live and not die, nor let his people be few."

Shiphrah and Puah

EX. 1:15–21

Shiphrah and Puah were Hebrew midwives in Egypt who were ordered by Pharaoh to kill the Hebrew boys when they were born. These women did not obey Pharaoh because they feared God, and God rewarded them.

Sihon the Amorite

NUM. 21; DEUT. 2

Sihon was the king of Heshbon who did not let Israel peacefully pass through his country. Because of his stubbornness, he was killed by the Israelites alongside everyone in Heshbon.

Simeon (Tribe)

NUM. 1:22–23; 2:12–13; 26:12–14

This tribe was descended from Jacob's son Simeon. The tribe suffered a significant decrease in population between the two censuses. Simeon is notable for being the only tribe that Moses did not bless before his death.

Zebulun (Tribe)

NUM. 1:30–31; 2:7–8; 26:26–27; DEUT. 33:18–19

This tribe was descended from Jacob's son Zebulun. The tribe's population increased between the two censuses. Moses blessed Zebulun and Issachar together saying, "They will feast on the abundance of the seas, on the treasures hidden in the sand."

Zelophehad's Daughters

NUM. 27:1–8; 36

Zelophehad's daughters—Mahlah, Noah, Hoglah, Milkah, and Tirzah—asked Moses to grant them their father's property as an inheritance. When

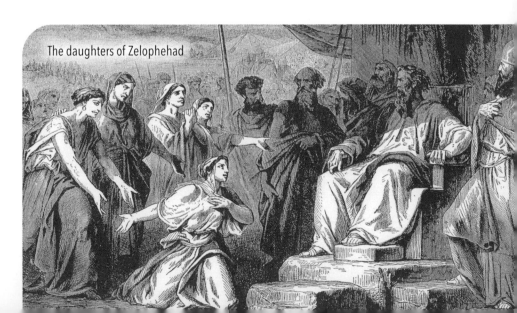

The daughters of Zelophehad

Moses went to God, the Lord decreed, "If a man dies and leaves no son, give his inheritance to his daughter." The one stipulation was that the daughters must marry within their own tribe, so the tribe would not lose its ancestral inheritance over the land.

Zipporah

EX. 2:21–22; 4:20–26; 18:2–6

Moses's wife Zipporah was one of Jethro's seven daughters in Midian. On her and Moses's journey to Egypt, Zipporah took the initiative to circumcise their firstborn son in accordance with the Abrahamic covenant. After Moses led the Israelites out of Egypt, she and her sons joined Moses in the desert.

Zipporah

CHAPTER 5

The Tabernacle

The tabernacle was a movable tent that God commanded Moses to build according to very specific instructions. The tribes of Israel took this tent and all its sacred items with them wherever they traveled in the wilderness. They set up the tabernacle in the center of their encampment. The tabernacle became:

- ✠ a visible expression of Israel's faith;

- ✠ a representation of a fundamental truth about God: he desires to live among his people; and

- ✠ a way for God to demonstrate his plan to intervene in human history to fix a broken creation.

From the beginning in the garden of Eden, God showed his desire to dwell with his creation and have a relationship with human beings. But sin corrupts and makes people impure; it separates humankind from God.

GOD'S PRESENCE BY DAY AND NIGHT

In the wilderness, the Lord manifested his presence with a cloud by day and a pillar of fire by night. This cloud or pillar would rest above the tabernacle, directly over the ark of the covenant. When the cloud or pillar moved, the people followed it in the wilderness. Wherever it stopped, they camped there until it moved again (Ex. 25:8, 22; 29:43; 40:34–38).

> But your iniquities have separated you from your God; your sins have hidden his face from you, so that he will not hear.
>
> ISAIAH 59:2

So how can a holy God dwell among a sinful people? The tabernacle was God's answer to this question. The tent, its sacred objects, the courtyard, and the activities performed within the tabernacle help us understand how God made a way his people in the wilderness to approach him and be with him.

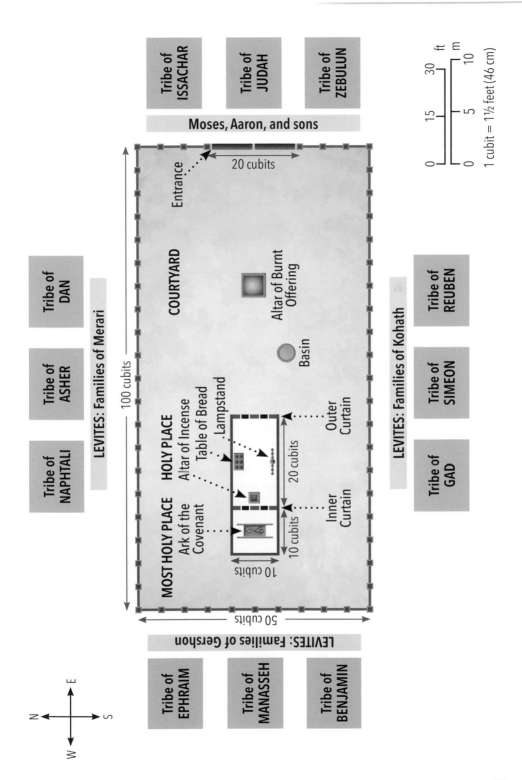

Tribe of ISSACHAR

Tribe of JUDAH

Tribe of ZEBULUN

Moses, Aaron, and sons

Entrance

20 cubits

COURTYARD

Tribe of DAN

Tribe of ASHER

Tribe of NAPHTALI

LEVITES: Families of Merari

100 cubits

Altar of Burnt Offering

Basin

HOLY PLACE

Altar of Incense
Table of Bread
Lampstand

MOST HOLY PLACE

Ark of the Covenant

Outer Curtain

20 cubits

Inner Curtain

10 cubits

10 cubits

50 cubits

LEVITES: Families of Kohath

Tribe of REUBEN

Tribe of SIMEON

Tribe of GAD

LEVITES: Families of Gershon

Tribe of EPHRAIM

Tribe of MANASSEH

Tribe of BENJAMIN

N E S W

30 ft
15
0

10 m
5
0

1 cubit = 1½ feet (46 cm)

THE COURTYARD

The courtyard of the tabernacle was enclosed by a fence made of a long piece of linen held up by posts. Only priests from the tribe of Levi were allowed to touch the tabernacle, so the fence protected people from accidentally venturing too close.

The fence was crafted from linen curtains, pillars, sockets, hooks, and fillets (tops and rods). Bronze pins held the linen curtains in place. A person would enter the courtyard through the one opening in the fence on the east side. The entrance had hanging curtains (blue, purple, scarlet, white), four pillars of brass, sockets of bronze (or brass), and hooks and fillets of silver on the tops of the pillars.

> ### CUBIT
>
> A cubit was an ancient unit of length. Though the exact size of a cubit varied in the ancient world, one cubit was approximately 18 inches (46 cm).

Instructions for the courtyard: Ex. 27:9–18; 38:9–20; 40:33

Size of the courtyard:

	CUBITS	FEET	METERS
LENGTH	100	150	46
WIDTH	50	75	23
HEIGHT	5	7.5	2.3

Who Were the Levites and Priests?

The Levites were one of the twelve tribes of Israel. Levi, the third son of Jacob, was the ancestor of the clan. This was the tribe that Moses, Aaron, and Miriam belonged to. Because of this tribe's zeal to protect the purity and worship of God, the Levites obtained special status as the priestly tribe (Ex. 32:25–29).

The Levites were responsible for keeping the tabernacle stocked with animals, grains, wine, wood, and everything necessary for the worship services. God also directed the Levites to assist the priests (Num. 3:5–10).

Three Levite families in particular were responsible for overseeing specific duties:

✠ The family of Gershon was in charge of the curtains of the tabernacle and courtyard (Num. 3:25–26).

✠ The family of Kohath was responsible for the furniture of the tabernacle, including the vessels and the curtains of the inner rooms (Num. 3:30–31).

✠ The family of Merari oversaw the tabernacle frames, bars, pillars, bases, and accessories (Num. 3:36).

Among the Levites, Aaron and his sons were especially set apart for the duties of the priesthood. God's intention was to make the entire nation of Israel a "kingdom of priests and a holy nation" to the world (Ex. 19:6). Within this nation, Aaron and his descendants would function as leaders (Ex. 19:22–24; 28:1–29:46).

Aaron and his sons were the only ones allowed to approach God.

> Appoint Aaron and his sons to serve as priests; anyone else who approaches the sanctuary [tabernacle] is to be put to death.
>
> NUMBERS 3:10

Also, only the sons of Aaron could become high priests. There was to be one high priest at any given time, but exceptions did occur in Israelite history, such as during the early monarchy when Zadok and Abiathar shared the office (2 Sam. 20:25). The office of high priest was hereditary and generally fell to the oldest son, unless some impediment disqualified him. Reasons for disqualification could include moral fault, ritual impurity, or physical deformity (Lev. 21:10–24). The high priest was also in charge of the entire priestly order and had oversight of the Levites as well (Num. 3; 8:14–22).

THE ALTAR OF BURNT OFFERING

Inside the courtyard, sacrifices were made on the altar of burnt offering, also called the bronze altar. This altar was made of acacia (shittim) wood and covered with bronze. Its four corners were adorned with horns. There were bronze shovels, basins, fleshhooks (forks), and fire pans to collect ashes. A bronze grate with a ring in each corner was put under the altar. Poles made of acacia wood covered with bronze were used to carry the altar when the Israelites journeyed through the wilderness.

Instructions for the altar of burnt offering: Ex. 27:1–8; 40:6, 10, 29

Size of the altar of burnt offering:

	CUBITS	FEET	METERS
LENGTH	5	7.5	2.3
WIDTH	5	7.5	2.3
HEIGHT	3	4.5	1.4

What Were the Offerings?

The altar was used for both animal (cattle, sheep, goats, doves) and meal offerings. While all types of offerings in some way symbolized communion between God and humans, the different offerings had their own specific purposes.

Sin Offering and Guilt Offering

Sin offerings and guilt offerings focused on paying for sin. The sin offering atoned for sins against God. The guilt offering was given for sins against others and included paying damages with interest. Various animals were sacrificed, depending on the person's position and income. Priests and leaders, as examples to others, had to offer larger sacrifices for their sins, while the poor offered what they could afford. The sacrificed animal's blood was sprinkled inside the first room of the tabernacle (the Holy Place) and poured on the altar of incense, with some blood smeared on the horns of the altar of incense.

The parts of the animal were burned, often with wine poured on them (a drink offering). In some cases, the meat could be eaten by the priests. Since priests were full-time tabernacle workers, sacrificed animals were their main source of food.

Instructions for the sin and guilt offering: Lev. 4–6; Num. 15:1–12

Burnt Offering

The burnt offering represented complete dedication and surrender to God. The animal, the best of the flock, bore the worshiper's sins and died in his or her place. After the animal's blood was sprinkled on the altar of burnt offering, its remains were completely burned. No part of the animal was roasted for eating.

Instructions for the burnt offering: Lev. 1:1–17

Grain Offering

The grain offering, also called the meal offering, was given to God in thankfulness. The people brought fine flour, unleavened cakes, or roasted grain to the priests. The priests burned a symbolic handful at the altar of burnt offering and could partake of the rest. There was very little ceremony involved.

Instructions for the grain offering: Lev. 2:1–16

Fellowship Offering

The fellowship offering, also called the peace offering, symbolized communion and harmony with God. After some meat was ceremonially waved toward heaven and given to the priests, worshipers and their guests would share in the feast as a meal with God.

Instructions for the fellowship offering: Lev. 3:1–17; 7:11–38

Why Sacrifices?

The sacrificial system in the Old Testament was part of the Mosaic law. Performing the rituals and sacrifices was an act of obedience, trust, and repentance:

- ✠ Obedience occurred by following God's very detailed commands about sacrifices.

- ✠ Trust existed because the person making the offering would have to trust God to provide the animals, which were expensive and a large portion of ancient Israel's livelihood.

- ✠ True repentance of the heart was supposed to accompany the sacrifices so they would not be hollow rituals.

The sacrifices also existed because of God's grace. They were God's merciful provision for his people so that their sin could be atoned for and God's holy presence could be in their midst.

One of the greatest problems people today have with the idea of sacrifice is its inevitable bloodiness. To many, sacrifices simply appear primitive and cruel. A brief word about how Old Testament people understood the concept of blood will be helpful for understanding their sacrifices.

In the Bible, the first encounter with blood occurs when Cain struck his brother Abel dead. God voices the seriousness of Cain's offense: "What have you done? Listen! Your brother's blood cries out to me from the ground" (Gen. 4:10). Then, in Genesis 9:3–6, God prohibits eating or drinking the blood of animals. The explanation for this is in Leviticus 17:

> For the life of a creature is in the blood, and I have given it to you to make atonement for yourselves on the altar; it is the blood that makes atonement for one's life.
>
> LEVITICUS 17:11

The blood of animals had a purpose: atonement.

Still, the question remains: why sacrifice animals? Remember the apostle Paul's words regarding sin: "For the wages of sin is death" (Rom. 6:23). Also keep in mind that the regulations for sacrifices occur in the context of the tabernacle. Animals became substitutes for humans: a life, an innocent life, for another's life, the life of a guilty one. Animal sacrifice,

then, was God's provision for sinful humans. The shedding of blood for the purifying or atoning rituals at the tabernacle reminded the worshiper that a life had been taken: the cost of sin is high indeed.

Because these sacrifices only temporarily covered the sins of the people, they needed to be offered on a regular basis. People would bring the offering to the tabernacle and put their hand on the head of the animal while it was killed. This symbolically, yet temporarily, transferred their sins onto the animal, and the animal died in their place.

The Old Testament sacrifices foreshadowed Jesus Christ, the far greater, perfect sacrifice who atoned for sin once and for all.

> First he [Christ] said, "Sacrifices and offerings, burnt offerings and sin offerings you did not desire, nor were you pleased with them"—though they were offered in accordance with the law. Then he said, "Here I am, I have come to do your will." He sets aside the first to establish the second. And by that will, we have been made holy through the sacrifice of the body of Jesus Christ once for all.
>
> HEBREWS 10:8–10

Jesus's sacrifice of himself on the cross made the Old Testament sacrificial system obsolete, as he ushered in the new covenant.

	OLD COVENANT	NEW COVENANT
TYPE OF SACRIFICE	Blood of animals Ex. 12:5; Lev. 1–7	Blood of Jesus Heb. 9:12; 13:12; 1 John 1:7
QUALITY OF SACRIFICE	Not enough; offered over and over Lev. 1–7; Heb. 9:7–9; 10:4	Enough; offered just once Heb. 9:12, 26
QUANTITY OF SACRIFICE	Many Lev. 1–7; Heb. 10:1	One Heb. 9:25–26
EFFECTIVENESS	For a day; for a year Ex. 29–30; Heb. 10:1–4	Forever Heb. 7:26–27; 9:12–15
ACTION OR RESULT	Temporary Ex. 30:10; Heb. 9:25	Final Rom. 6:10; Heb. 9:25–28

THE BASIN

After the sacrifice was made, the rest of the steps done at the tabernacle were performed by the priests on behalf of the people. Once a priest completed the sacrifice, he washed his hands and feet with water from the basin, also called the laver. This washing purified the priest and prepared him to enter into the tabernacle.

The basin was made from brass mirrors donated by the women of Israel. It may have had a shiny mirrored surface which would help the priest wash thoroughly and remind him that the Lord sees past the outward appearance, straight into the heart.

Instructions for the basin: Ex. 30:17–21; 40:7, 30–32

The size of the basin is unknown.

What Was Purity in the Old Testament?

The issue of purity, or cleanliness, was very important for the ancient Israelites. In Old Testament times, cleanliness meant something different than how we think of it today. In the Mosaic law, the holy and the impure cannot coexist, and God provided a means to cleanse what had become impure. He chose purification rites and sacrifices to undo impurity. The priestly ritual of washing hands and feet with water from the tabernacle basin is one such example.

There are two main categories of impurity in the Old Testament: ritual and moral.

	RITUAL IMPURITY	MORAL IMPURITY
KIND	Unavoidable, since it was part of life. It was not sinful.	Avoidable. It was directly linked to human sin and disobedience.
CAUSES	Entry of foreign entities into the body (Lev. 11:39–40); contact with unclean things (Lev. 11:24–31); skin diseases (Lev. 13:1–46); loss of bodily fluids (Lev. 12:2; 15)	Idolatry (Lev. 18:21; 19:31) and certain sexual transgressions (Lev. 18:6–18; 20:11–14)
CONSEQUENCES	Impurity was contagious and inevitable. The Israelites had to be aware of their condition and take steps to avoid contamination. Impurity excluded people from worshiping at the tabernacle or even remaining in the camp (example: Num. 12:10–15).	Moral impurity was not contagious by touch. However, its effects were broad: they contaminated the individual, the land, and the tabernacle.
DURATION	Temporary and short-term	Temporary but long-lasting effects
UNDOING	Ritual bathing, offering or sacrifice, waiting for a set period of time	Atonement, punishment, exile, or even death

Jesus changed this situation. The different purification rites and sacrifices in the Old Testament were anticipations of Christ's ministry. Because of the perfect cleansing in Jesus's blood and his ultimate sacrifice on the cross, the purification rites and sacrifices are no longer necessary.

During Jesus's ministry, he frequently chastised the Pharisees and teachers of the law for focusing so much on outward obedience to purity rituals, while ignoring the impurity in their hearts:

> Woe to you, teachers of the law and Pharisees, you hypocrites! You clean the outside of the cup and dish, but inside they are full of greed and self-indulgence. Blind Pharisee! First clean the inside of the cup and dish, and then the outside also will be clean.
>
> MATTHEW 23:25–26

THE TABERNACLE

The priests entered the tabernacle through one entrance covered by a curtain, also called the outer curtain or outer veil. The tabernacle structure was made of a goat hair covering with a linen covering beneath; a ram skin covering dyed red; a badger, porpoise, or sea cow skin covering; forty-eight boards; and one hundred sockets, along with bars, pillars, hooks, and curtains.

The tabernacle was divided into two rooms: the Holy Place and the Most Holy Place.

✠ The Holy Place, also called the Holy of Holies, was twenty cubits long, twice the size of the Most Holy Place. This larger room contained the table of the bread of the presence, the seven-branched golden lampstand, and the altar of incense which sat in front of the inner curtain between the two rooms. Every day, priests entered the Holy Place to serve the Lord.

✠ The smaller room, the Most Holy Place, was the most sacred spot in the tabernacle, because it contained the ark of the covenant. The high priest entered this room only once a year on the Day of Atonement.

Instructions for the tabernacle: Ex. 25:1–9; 26:1–37

Size of the tabernacle:

	CUBITS	FEET	METERS
LENGTH	30	45	13.8
WIDTH	10	15	4.6
HEIGHT	10	15	4.6

THE LAMPSTAND

The lampstand stood in the Holy Place and provided light in this otherwise dark room. Priests trimmed the wicks to keep them burning brightly. The lampstand was made from a single piece of gold; it was not pieced together. It had a central shaft with six branches, three on each side, making it a seven-branched lampstand. Each branch had knobs, flowers, and an almond-shaped bowl to hold pure olive oil.

Instructions for the lampstand: Ex. 25:31–40

The size of the lampstand is unknown.

THE TABLE OF THE BREAD OF PRESENCE

On the table of the bread of the presence (also called the table of showbread) were twelve loaves of bread made from fine flour, representing the twelve tribes of Israel. The loaves were a continual reminder of the everlasting promises between God and the Israelites, and they served as a memorial of God's provision of food in the wilderness.

This small table was made of acacia wood, overlaid with gold, and had a crown or frame of gold around it. Gold carrying poles were put through rings on the corners of the table. There were also gold dishes, pans, pitchers, and bowls.

The bread on the table was eaten by the high priest and his sons. The bread was replaced every week on the Sabbath.

Instructions for the table: Ex. 25:23–30

Size of the table:

	CUBITS	INCHES	CENTIMETERS
LENGTH	2	36	92
WIDTH	1	18	46
HEIGHT	1.5	27	69

ACACIA WOOD

Acacia wood is a hard wood that insects find distasteful. It is also a dense wood, which protects it from decay and water damage. This made it an ideal wood for constructing and preserving the tabernacle and its furnishings, which were frequently moved in the wilderness journey.

THE ALTAR OF INCENSE

The high priest burned incense on this small altar in the Holy Place every morning and evening. The altar was made from acacia wood covered in

gold. It had four corners, each with a horn, and a crown or molding along the edges. Once a year on the Day of Atonement, the horns of the altar were sprinkled with the blood of the sin offering.

The Lord required that special incense be burned constantly on the altar. It was a unique, sweet incense, a mixture of spices to be used only for the tabernacle. God specifically required this—and only this— recipe. The incense was a matter of life and death, as Leviticus 10:1–2 clearly shows when two of Aaron's sons offered an "unauthorized fire" before the Lord and were struck dead.

Instructions for the altar: Ex. 30:1–10, 34–37

Size of the altar:

	CUBITS	INCHES	CENTIMETERS
LENGTH	1	18	46
WIDTH	1	18	46
HEIGHT	2	36	92

THE INNER CURTAIN

The inner curtain, also called the veil, separated the two rooms of the tabernacle. Symbolically, this curtain was a barrier between God and humanity. Only the high priest was allowed to enter through the curtain and into the Most Holy Place where the ark of the covenant was kept.

The curtain was made of heavy woven cloth. There was no separation in the middle, so the high priest had to go around the side. It was hung on four pillars of acacia wood overlaid with gold. Four gold hooks were put in four sockets of silver. It was made of blue, purple, and scarlet threads and had designs of cherubim embroidered on it.

Instructions for the inner curtain: Ex. 26:31–33

Size of the inner curtain:

	CUBITS	FEET	METERS
WIDTH	10	15	4.6
HEIGHT	10	15	4.6

CHERUBIM

Cherubim are angelic beings who protect God's glory, keeping unholy things out of his presence. They protected the garden of Eden, barring the way into God's presence after Adam and Eve sinned (Gen. 3:24). Cherubim also flank or support God's throne in heaven (Isa. 37:16; Ezek. 10:1–22). Images of cherubim in the tabernacle would have served as a reminder about heavenly realities: God's holiness and the separation that existed between God and humankind.

A New Way to God

Later in Israel's history, the temple built in Jerusalem took the place of the tabernacle. The curtain in the temple followed a similar design to the one in the tabernacle. When Jesus breathed his last breath on the cross, the thick curtain of the temple tore from top to bottom. This symbolized the ability of every believer, not just a high priest, to approach God. The writer of the book of Hebrews explains it this way:

> Since we have confidence to enter the Most Holy Place by the blood of Jesus, by a new and living way opened for us through the curtain, that is, his body, and since we have a great priest over the house of God, let us draw near to God with a sincere heart and with the full assurance that faith brings.
>
> HEBREWS 10:19–22

THE ARK OF THE COVENANT

The ark of the covenant was the most sacred object of ancient Israel. This small, gold, box-like item became a powerful symbol of God's power, guidance, and mercy among his people. It was at the ark that God told Moses that he would meet Moses and provide "all [his] commands for the Israelites" (Ex. 25:22).

The Bible lists the ark as the first item Moses and the Israelites constructed for the tabernacle. Built in the shape of a rectangular box, it was made of

acacia wood and covered in pure gold both inside and outside. Four rings of gold were attached to the ark, through which two poles were placed so that it could be carried. The poles were also made of acacia wood and overlaid with gold. These poles were never to be removed from the rings on the ark.

The lid of the ark was called the mercy seat or atonement cover. The mercy seat is referred to more than twenty times in the Bible. This top (or lid) was made of pure gold, and above it were two cherubim figures made of hammered gold whose wings overshadowed it.

God promised to be present upon the mercy seat, especially during the annual Day of Atonement when the high priest made a sacrifice for the sins of the people (Ex. 30:6; Lev. 16:2). On this day, the high priest would bring two animals, usually goats, to the tabernacle courtyard. He sacrificed one of the goats and sprinkled its blood on the mercy seat. He placed his hands on the other goat and prayed for God's forgiveness for all the sins of the people. Their sins were symbolically transferred onto the animal which was then released into the wilderness. This "scapegoat" was a visual representation of the people's sins being carried away, never to return.

Instructions for the ark: Ex. 25:10–22

Size of the ark:

	CUBITS	INCHES	CENTIMETERS
LENGTH	2.5	45	115
WIDTH	1.5	27	69
HEIGHT	1.5	27	69

NAMES FOR THE ARK

"Ark of the covenant" in Hebrew is *aron haberit*. *Aron* means "chest" or "box," and it is even translated as "coffin" in Genesis 50:26, discussing Joseph's burial in Egypt. In the Bible, the ark of the covenant is also referred to as the ark of God (1 Sam. 3:3), the ark of the Sovereign Lord (1 Kings 2:26), the sacred ark (2 Chron. 35:3), the ark of your might (Ps. 132:8), and the ark of the covenant law or testimony (Ex. 25:22).

What Was Inside the Ark?

The ark contained three things:

> "... the gold jar of manna, Aaron's staff that had budded, and the stone tablets of the covenant."

HEBREWS 9:4

Gold Jar of Manna

✠ God provided manna for the Israelites for forty years in the wilderness until they entered the promised land (Ex. 16:35; Josh. 5:12). Manna was a substance like coriander and the color of gum resin (Num. 11:7). It was crushed, boiled, and baked, and tasted like cakes with oil or honey (Ex. 16:23, 31; Num. 11:8). *Manna* translated means "what is it?"

✠ Moses commanded that a jar of manna be kept through the ages to remind the Israelites of how God had provided for them (Ex. 16:33).

✠ Manna is used symbolically in the Bible to show God's provision (Neh. 9:20; Deut. 8:3; John 6:31; Rev. 2:17).

Aaron's Staff

✠ To put an end to a revolt against Moses and Aaron, God instructed staffs from the leaders of the tribes to be placed before the ark. God caused Aaron's staff to bud, sprout, and produce almonds, confirming that he had selected Aaron and the tribe of Levi to serve as priests to lead the people (Num. 17:1–8).

✠ Aaron's staff became a reminder to stop further rebellions. It was kept in front of the ark, and at times inside (Num. 17:10; Heb. 9:4).

Tablets of the Covenant

✠ The ark contained the stone tablets (the Ten Commandments) of the covenant between God and Israel (Deut. 10:1–5). They were to remind the Israelites of God's holy nature and his covenant promise with them.

✠ In the ancient Near East, kings would often keep a copy of the kingdom's laws at the foot of their throne to remind both the people and the king of their covenant. Archaeological evidence has revealed that Israel's ark looked remarkably similar to ancient footstools of royal thrones. Scripture alludes to the idea of the ark as God's footstool (Ps. 132:7–8; 1 Chron. 28:2). By the time of Solomon, a few centuries after Moses, the only thing that remained inside the ark was the two stone tablets (1 Kings 8:9).

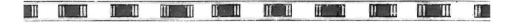

THE ARK AND THE POWER OF GOD'S PRESENCE

The ark of the covenant, as the visual representation of God's presence, traveled ahead of the Israelites on their way to the promised land. Once the people arrived at the Jordan River to enter Canaan, Joshua, Moses's successor, ordered the Levites to carry the ark across the river first. The Levites took the ark through the river on dry ground, reminiscent of the crossing of the sea in the exodus: "As soon as the priests who carried the ark reached the Jordan and their feet touched the water's edge, the water from upstream stopped flowing.... The priests who carried the ark of the covenant of the Lord stopped in the middle of the Jordan and stood on dry ground, while all Israel passed by until the whole nation had completed the crossing on dry ground" (Josh. 3:15–17). God, the great King, was leading his army.

ARK OF THE COVENANT TIMELINE

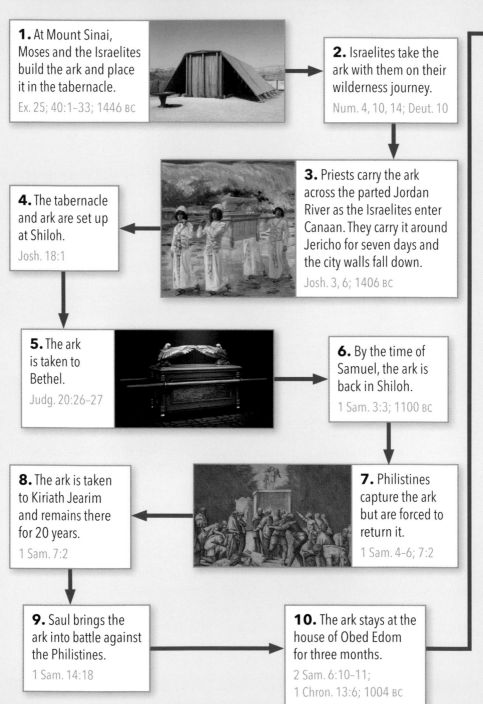

1. At Mount Sinai, Moses and the Israelites build the ark and place it in the tabernacle.

Ex. 25; 40:1–33; 1446 BC

2. Israelites take the ark with them on their wilderness journey.

Num. 4, 10, 14; Deut. 10

3. Priests carry the ark across the parted Jordan River as the Israelites enter Canaan. They carry it around Jericho for seven days and the city walls fall down.

Josh. 3, 6; 1406 BC

4. The tabernacle and ark are set up at Shiloh.

Josh. 18:1

5. The ark is taken to Bethel.

Judg. 20:26–27

6. By the time of Samuel, the ark is back in Shiloh.

1 Sam. 3:3; 1100 BC

7. Philistines capture the ark but are forced to return it.

1 Sam. 4–6; 7:2

8. The ark is taken to Kiriath Jearim and remains there for 20 years.

1 Sam. 7:2

9. Saul brings the ark into battle against the Philistines.

1 Sam. 14:18

10. The ark stays at the house of Obed Edom for three months.

2 Sam. 6:10–11; 1 Chron. 13:6; 1004 BC

11. King David brings the ark to Jerusalem.

2 Sam. 6:1–15; 1004 BC

12. King Solomon builds the temple in Jerusalem and places the ark in the temple's Most Holy Place.

1 Kings 8:1–9; 2 Chron. 5:2–10; 960 BC

14. Jeremiah prophesies that one day "people will no longer say, 'The ark of the covenant of the LORD.' It will never enter their minds or be remembered; it will not be missed, nor will another one be made."

Jer. 3:16

13. By the time of King Josiah, the ark is no longer in the temple. Josiah discovers the book of the law and orders the ark to be put back in the temple. (This is the last mention in the Bible of the ark's whereabouts.)

2 Chron. 35:3; 623 BC

15. Babylonians invade Jerusalem and burn the temple. It's believed the ark was either destroyed or carried off into Babylon with other sacred temple items.

2 Kings 25:13–17; 586 BC

17. By the time of Jesus, there is still no ark in the temple. The last mention of the ark in the Bible is in John's vision of the temple of God in heaven.

Rev. 11:19

16. The exiles return to Jerusalem and rebuild the temple, but there is no mention of the ark.

Ezra 4:11–12; 6:15; 516 BC

What Happened to the Ark?

The last historical reference to the ark was when King Josiah instructed the Levites to return it to the temple (2 Chron. 35:1–6). Nothing is said about why the ark had been removed, who moved it, where it had been taken, or if it actually was brought back. Throughout the centuries, many different theories for what happened to the ark have been proposed. Here are a few of the main ones:

Ethiopia

It has been suggested that after the queen of Sheba visited King Solomon in Jerusalem (1 Kings 10:1–13; 2 Chron. 9:1–12), Solomon married her—though Scripture says nothing about such a marriage. The ark was then smuggled into Ethiopia by Menelik, the alleged son of Solomon and the queen of Sheba. The ark is now supposedly located at St. Mary of Zion Orthodox Church in Axum, Ethiopia. However, no independent source has been allowed to view the ark to verify its authenticity.

St. Mary of Zion Orthodox Church

Egypt

One theory says that the ark was taken by Pharaoh Shishak of Egypt when he attacked Jerusalem in the tenth century BC. The Bible says that the pharaoh carried off the temple treasures but does not specifically mention the ark (1 Kings 14:25–26; 2 Chron. 12:9).

Mount Nebo

In the apocryphal book of 2 Maccabees, it is said that the prophet Jeremiah received a revelation instructing him to take the ark to Mount Nebo (today in Jordan). Jeremiah then found a room in a cave on or near Mount Nebo in which he placed the ark and sealed the entrance. The ark's exact location will be divinely revealed at an appointed time. While the accuracy of this account is certainly debated, Jeremiah was from a priestly family which would have provided him access to the ark, and he had prophesied that there would come a time when the ark would no longer be needed (Jer. 1:1; 3:16).

Dome of the Rock on the Temple Mount

Temple Mount

Some claim that priests hid the ark by burying it under the Temple Mount in Jerusalem sometime during the Babylonian siege of the city in the sixth century BC. However, the area is inaccessible today because this location is currently the site of the Dome of the Rock, an Islamic shrine.

Mount Gerizim

First-century historian, Josephus, mentions a Samaritan tradition that says the "sacred vessels" were hidden on Mount Gerizim (today in the West Bank). While the ark is not expressly mentioned, tradition holds that the ark was part of this collection.

Babylon

When the Babylonians conquered Jerusalem and set fire to the temple in 586 BC, it is believed they took the ark to Babylon (today in Iraq) where it disappeared or was destroyed (2 Kings 24:13; 2 Chron. 36:5–8). Curiously, the ark is not listed among the spoils (2 Kings 25:13–18; Jer. 52:17–23). (Though it would be surprising if they took the pots and shovels of the temple but left behind a valuable item like the ark.) When the Israelites returned from exile, the list of items that were brought back to Judah makes no mention of the ark (Ezra 1:5–11).

It is important to remember that even though the discovery of the ark would be an incredible historical and archaeological find, the ark itself has no supernatural powers. It was only God's presence associated with the ark that gave it importance. According to the New Testament, God's Spirit is now within every person who believes in his son Jesus Christ (Rom. 8:11).

CHAPTER 6

Passover and Other Feasts

When God freed Israel from Egypt, he made his purposes clear: to show that he alone is the true and mighty God, Creator of heaven and earth; to make Israel's descendants his own people, his treasured possession; to have a people who worshiped him as the only God; and to keep his promise to Abraham to make his descendants great and many, giving them a land flowing with milk and honey.

The people of Israel were a worshiping people. In fact, Moses's message from God to Pharaoh was to let the people leave so they could go and worship God:

> The LORD, the God of the Hebrews, has sent me to say to you: "Let my people go, so that they may worship me in the wilderness."
>
> EXODUS 7:16

Once liberated from slavery and living in the wilderness, Israel came to understand God's centrality to their lives. He was at the center of their camp, his presence represented by the tabernacle. The Israelites organized their lives around God's presence: their movements, their festivals, and their daily routines. Their worship was a recognition of their total dependence on God. Their life in the wilderness was a life of faith—faith that God would provide food, water, and security from the dangers of the desert.

A large section of the Pentateuch (the first five books of the Old Testament) deals with matters of worship expressed through rituals, sacrifices, prayers, and special feasts. There were seven feasts that God instituted as times for his people to meet with him and worship him. The Lord told Moses, "Speak to the Israelites and say to them: These are my appointed festivals, the appointed festivals of the LORD, which you are to proclaim as sacred assemblies" (Lev. 23:1–2).

The Appointed Feasts

	BIBLICAL FEAST	OTHER NAMES	SCRIPTURE
1	**Passover**	Pesach	Ex. 12:1–14 Lev. 23:4–5
2	**Feast of Unleavened Bread***	Hag HaMatzot	Ex. 12:15–20 Lev. 23:6–8
3	**Firstfruits**	Reishit	Lev. 23:9–14
4	**Feast of Weeks***	Shavuot, Pentecost	Lev. 23:15–22
5	**Feast of Trumpets**	Yom HaTeruah Rosh HaShanah	Lev. 23:23–25
6	**Day of Atonement**	Yom Kippur	Lev. 23:26–32
7	**Feast of Booths***	Feast of Tabernacles Sukkot	Lev. 23:33–43

*Pilgrimage feast

The seven appointed feasts were to be a time for remembering, resting (sabbath), giving thanks, repenting, offering sacrifices, and reading the Scriptures.

Once the generation after Moses settled in the promised land, three of the seven feasts were celebrated as pilgrimage feasts when all Jewish males went to Jerusalem to "appear before the LORD" (Deut. 16:16): the Feast of Unleavened Bread, the Feast of Weeks, and the Feast of Booths.

THE CALENDAR

Although many feasts originated in the wilderness and were observed around the tabernacle, their unique traditions developed over Israel's long history. Other holidays were also added to the calendar, for example, Purim and Hanukkah. (See Esther 9 for the origin of Purim.)

As the first Passover was about to happen before the Israelites left Egypt, God established the order of the months for his people.

> The LORD said to Moses and Aaron in Egypt, "This month is to be for you the first month, the first month of your year."
>
> EXODUS 12:1

This was the first Jewish calendar used to determine the holidays, or the religious year. Following the Babylonian exile in the sixth century BC, the Jewish calendar reflected Babylonian names for the months. For example, the first month of the year, in which Passover was observed, is called Aviv (Abib) in the book of Exodus (Ex. 13:4), but it is called Nisan later in Israel's history after the exile (Neh. 2:1). These later names still exist in the Jewish calendar today.

Israel observed each of the seven appointed feasts once a year. Every month, they also celebrated the "new moon" which marked the beginning of the month: "… and New Moon feasts—you are to sound the trumpets over your burnt offerings and fellowship offerings, and they will be a memorial for you before your God" (Num. 10:10). Weekly, the people observed the seventh day as a day of rest, the Sabbath (Shabbat): "Remember the Sabbath day by keeping it holy. Six days you shall labor and do all your work, but the seventh day is a sabbath to the LORD your God" (Ex. 20:8–10). The Jewish day began at sunset.

The yearly cycles of sowing and harvesting were very important to ancient Israel. From an agricultural perspective, the three pilgrimage feasts corresponded to Israel's harvest seasons:

- ✠ The Feast of Unleavened Bread during the barley harvest (early spring)

- ✠ The Feast of Weeks during the wheat harvest (late spring)

- ✠ The Feast of Booths during the fruit harvest (early autumn)

Today, there are twelve months in the Jewish calendar, each with twenty-nine or thirty days. Approximately every third year is a leap year containing an extra month. This adjustment is necessary to ensure that the major festivals stay in their appointed seasons. The Jewish calendar now is determined by precise astronomical calculations, but for centuries the calendar was determined each month by the sighting of the new moon (Ps. 81:3), Rosh Hodesh ("head of the month"). The new moon is still observed, nowadays in synagogues with prayers, Scripture readings, and special greetings.

The calendar used by most western nations today is called the Gregorian calendar (January–December). It was established by Pope Gregory VIII in 1582. It is a solar calendar. The Jewish calendar, however, uses both lunar and solar movements. The months are determined by the moon, and the year is determined by the sun.

By the time of Jesus in the first century AD, there was a second calendar used for civil affairs. This calendar began with the month of Tishri (September/October). The first of Tishri was (and still is) the civil New Year, Rosh HaShanah. This second calendar is still in use today.

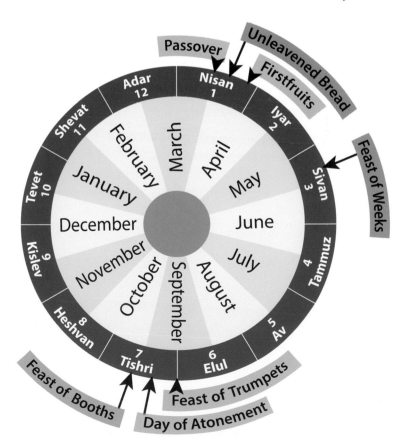

PASSOVER

Passover commemorated the Israelites' deliverance from slavery in Egypt. It was the first feast observed in the religious year.

After sending nine plagues upon Egypt, the Lord said the firstborn males of every house would die unless the doorframe of that house was covered with the blood of a perfect lamb. On the night of the plague, the Lord "passed over" the homes with blood on the doorframes, sparing the firstborns within. After this plague, Pharaoh let the Israelites leave.

Passover was to be observed for generations to come:

> This is a day you are to commemorate; for the generations to come you shall celebrate it as a festival to the LORD— a lasting ordinance.
>
> EXODUS 12:14

Passover and Jesus Christ

In Exodus, God gave Israel detailed instructions about how to observe the Passover meal. The Passover foreshadowed Jesus Christ as "the Lamb of God who takes away the sin of the world!" (John 1:29).

PASSOVER	JESUS CHRIST
The feast marked a new year and a new beginning for God's people (Ex. 12:1–2).	In Christ, every believer is a new creation, and old things and the old life are past (2 Cor. 5:17).
A male lamb in its first year was taken into the home on the tenth of Nisan (the first month). It was closely inspected to see if it had any blemishes or disfigurements. If it was without defect, it was sacrificed on the fourteenth of Nisan (Ex. 12:5).	Christ was closely inspected by Pilate (Matt. 27:11–26), Herod (Luke 23:8–12), Annas (John 18:12–13), and Caiaphas (Matt. 26:57). They found no fault in him. Christ is the "lamb without blemish or defect" (1 Peter 1:19).
God commanded Israel not to break any bones of the sacrificed lamb (Ex. 12:46).	To speed up Jesus's death on the cross, the Roman soldiers were going to break his legs. However, Jesus was already dead, so his bones remained unbroken (John 19:32–33).
The blood of the lamb was applied to the door frame—the lintel and side posts. Because of the covering of blood, the house was spared from God's plague (Ex. 12:7, 12, 22).	We need to be covered or justified by the blood of the Lamb to be rescued from condemnation (Rom. 3:25; 5:9). Christ is the Lamb that takes away sins (John 1:29).
Passover was to be kept as a remembrance forever (Ex. 12:14).	During the Last Supper, Jesus referred to the bread as "my body given for you; do this in remembrance of me" (Luke 22:19).
The whole community of God's people was required to participate in the Passover sacrifice (Ex. 12:6).	Accepting Christ's sacrifice is required for all who want to be part of God's community (Rom. 3:21–26).

Fascinating Facts about Passover

✠ Jesus's parents traveled to Jerusalem yearly to celebrate Passover. At age twelve, Jesus went with them (Luke 2:41–50).

✠ The Passover was a celebration, remembrance, thanksgiving, and participation in God's mighty acts of salvation for his people. The New Testament equivalent of the Passover, the Lord's Supper, functions in similar ways for Christians today: it is a time of remembrance and thanksgiving (Luke 22:19; 1 Cor. 11:24–25); a time for refreshing and communion (Rom. 5:10; 1 Cor. 10:16); and a time for anticipation and recommitment (1 Cor. 11:26, 28–29).

✠ Today, the Passover meal (Seder) is observed with a plate containing various foods with symbolic meanings, including horseradish and lettuce symbolizing the bitterness of slavery in Egypt; parsley dipped in salt water symbolizing the tears and pain suffered by Israel; haroset, a sweet paste made of fruits and nuts, symbolizing the mortar used by the Israelite slaves to make bricks; and a roasted lamb shank recalling the sacrificed Passover lamb.

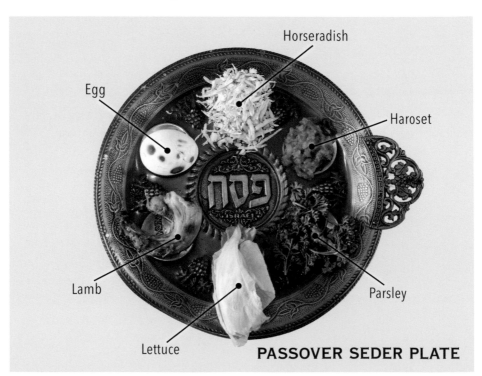

PASSOVER SEDER PLATE

FEAST OF UNLEAVENED BREAD

The Feast of Unleavened Bread commemorated Israel's escape from Egypt. The unleavened bread (matzah) was made in a hurry without yeast, representing how the Lord brought the Israelites out of Egypt in haste. The book of Leviticus mentions this feast as a separate feast on the fifteenth day of Nisan, the same month as Passover. The Lord commanded the Israelites to eat unleavened bread for seven days.

> On the fifteenth day of that month the LORD's Festival of Unleavened Bread begins; for seven days you must eat bread made without yeast.
>
> LEVITICUS 23:6

Today, the feasts of Passover, Unleavened Bread, and Firstfruits have all been incorporated into the celebration of Passover, which is observed for eight days. Additionally, the time of eating the unleavened bread has become a time of spiritual preparation. The Feast of Unleavened Bread symbolizes a time of renewal and cleansing.

Leaven in the Bible

Leaven is something added to bread to make it rise. In Bible times, a leftover piece of fermented dough was used to make a new batch of dough rise. (Today, yeast is used to leaven dough.) Leaven requires time to expand. Eating unleavened bread is a way to remember the haste with which God's people left Egypt (Ex. 12:14–20).

Leaven was prohibited only at Passover and in foods dedicated to the Lord by fire (Lev. 2:11). In the Passover, omitting leaven could represent a complete break from the previous life in Egypt and the coming into a new life under the Lord. For Israel's fellowship and bread offerings, however, leavened breads were required (Lev. 7:13; 23:17), suggesting that in the Old Testament, leaven does not always represent sin or something negative.

In the New Testament, leaven is used as a symbol of either good or bad influence. In Matthew 13:33, Jesus uses the image of leaven to explain the kingdom of heaven. Like leaven, the kingdom works unseen, powerfully, and relentlessly. In Luke 12:1, Jesus warns the disciples to beware of the Pharisees' teachings because, like leaven, they corrupt everything they touch. In 1 Corinthians 5:6–8, the apostle Paul uses leaven imagery to emphasize the effects of bad influence: it spreads quickly and quietly. In other words, "malice and wickedness" corrupt everything just as leaven spreads and transforms the whole lump of bread.

Unleavened Bread and Jesus

Unleavened bread can represent a pure life, a life without sin. Jesus is the only human without sin. Jesus said that the "bread of God is the bread that comes down from heaven and gives life to the world" (John 6:33). Jesus also declared, "I am the bread of life. Whoever comes to me will never go hungry" (John 6:35).

Today, when matzah (unleavened bread) is made, it is pierced so the dough will not rise with the heat. It is also striped with marks made by the cook ware. (In the past, however, matzah looked like pita bread.) Many Jewish Christians understand the piercing and the stripes to symbolize the piercing of Jesus on the cross and his flogging by the Roman soldiers (John 19:1, 34).

Fascinating Facts about the Feast of Unleavened Bread

- ✠ The only type of bread eaten during the eight days of Passover/Feast of Unleavened Bread is matzah. It is made with flour and water only. The utensils used must never touch leaven.

- ✠ Bakery goods during this festival are made with matzo meal.

- ✠ Orthodox Jews believe that during the feast even having leaven present in one's home is forbidden.

- ✠ Today, cleansing the house the night before Passover is often a symbolic search to remove any hypocrisy or wickedness.

Traditionally, the father searches for any leaven in the house. He sweeps any remaining bread crumbs onto a wooden spoon with a goose feather. The crumbs, spoon, and feather are placed in a bag and burned the next morning.

FIRSTFRUITS

The offering of firstfruits was a reminder to Israel that God was the source of their prosperity and welfare. Firstfruits were given for the spring barley harvest. The first ripe sheaf, called the firstfruits, of barley was offered to the Lord as an act of dedicating the harvest to him. It was a demonstration of thanksgiving and commitment.

> When you enter the land I am going to give you and you reap its harvest, bring to the priest a sheaf of the first grain you harvest. He is to wave the sheaf before the LORD so it will be accepted on your behalf.
>
> LEVITICUS 23:10–11

This presentation of firstfruits happened after Passover, on the third day:

✠ On Passover, a marked sheaf of grain was bundled and left standing in the field. (first day)

✠ The next day was the beginning of the Feast of Unleavened Bread, and it was on this day that the sheaf was cut and prepared for offering. (second day)

✠ Then on the following day, the priest waved the sheaf before the Lord. (third day)

The "counting of the days" then began and continued up to the day after the seventh Sabbath, the fiftieth day. This fiftieth day became known as Pentecost.

Firstfruits and Jesus

After the destruction of the Jerusalem temple in AD 70, Jewish people rarely celebrated Firstfruits. But for followers of Jesus, the day of Firstfruits has great significance because it is the day of Jesus's resurrection. Jesus rose on the third day of Passover season, the day of Firstfruits (Luke 24:46–47). His resurrection gave new meaning to this agricultural holiday, as the promise of the future resurrection of believers.

> But Christ has indeed been raised from the dead, the firstfruits of those who have fallen asleep. For since death came through a man, the resurrection of the dead comes also through a man. For as in Adam all die, so in Christ all will be made alive. But each in his own turn: Christ, the firstfruits; then, when he comes, those who belong to him.
>
> 1 CORINTHIANS 15:20–23

Fascinating Facts about Firstfruits

✠ The manna, which God provided from heaven as food for the Israelites in the wilderness, stopped on the day of Firstfruits after the people entered the promised land (Josh. 5:10–12).

✠ Today, Jews use this holiday to begin the counting of the days, also known as the "counting of the omer." An omer is a biblical measure of volume of grain, and in Hebrew it means "barley."

FEAST OF WEEKS

The Feast of Weeks celebrated God's provision of material blessings. Traditionally, this celebration marked the culmination of the events that began with Passover. Because it was an offering of grain of the summer wheat harvest presented to the Lord, it also became known as the Feast of Harvest or Latter Firstfruits.

> Count off fifty days up to the day after the seventh Sabbath, and then present an offering of new grain to the LORD.
>
> LEVITICUS 23:16

> Count off seven weeks from the time you begin to put the sickle to the standing grain. Then celebrate the Feast of Weeks to the LORD your God by giving a freewill offering in proportion to the blessings the LORD your God has given you.
>
> DEUTERONOMY 16:9–10

The Feast of Weeks was celebrated seven weeks from the third day after Passover (the day of Firstfruits), when the Israelites leaving Egypt arrived at Mount Sinai. Because of this connection, the Feast of Weeks is also a commemoration of the giving of the law (Torah). It is known as "the Season of the Giving of Torah," the time when God gave Moses the Ten Commandments.

Feast of Weeks and Jesus

After his resurrection, Jesus told his disciples to wait in Jerusalem. The disciples were all together in the upper room for the Feast of Weeks on the fiftieth day (Pentecost) after the Sabbath of Passover week—the first day of the week. Then the sound of a mighty wind filled the house and what appeared to be tongues of fire came to rest on the disciples, and they were filled with the Holy Spirit. The apostle Peter referred to the prophet Joel who said that God would "pour out his Spirit on all people" (Joel 2:28; Acts 2:32). God was fulfilling his promises right before their eyes. The people responded to Peter's message, and more than three thousand were baptized that day.

The covenant between God and Israel was initiated on the Feast of Weeks at the foot of Mount Sinai, seven weeks after the Passover miracle in Egypt. On the day of Pentecost, fifty days after the death of Christ, the Holy Spirit sealed the new covenant in Jesus's blood (2 Cor. 1:22; Eph. 1:13; 4:30).

Fascinating Facts about the Feast of Weeks

- ✠ This feast is called Shavuot, which in Hebrew means "weeks." Because Shavuot is celebrated fifty days after Passover, it also became known as Pentecost, meaning "fifty" in Greek.

- ✠ The days from Passover to Shavuot are counted at weekly Sabbath services.

- ✠ Historically, children receive treats for memorizing Scripture at Shavuot.

- ✠ The book of Ruth is often read.

- ✠ Special dairy desserts are prepared for this holiday because the Torah is compared to milk and honey.

- ✠ Homes and synagogues are decorated with flowers and greenery, representing the harvest and the Torah as a tree of life.

- ✠ Observant Jews often spend the night reading and studying Torah.

FEAST OF TRUMPETS

In biblical times, this day was a time of rest and offerings commemorated with trumpet blasts (Num. 29:1–6). The trumpet (or horn) was a shofar, a ram's horn. There are no other instructions given in Scripture for this holiday.

> On the first day of the seventh month you are to have a day of Sabbath rest, a sacred assembly commemorated with trumpet blasts. Do no regular work, but present a food offering to the LORD.
>
> LEVITICUS 23:23–25

Today, Rosh HaShanah is the first day of the seventh month (Tishrei) of the religious calendar. Rosh HaShanah means "the beginning of the year," because it marks the start of the Jewish civil new year. Rosh HaShanah, the Ten Days of Repentance that follow it, and then Yom Kippur (Day of Atonement) make up the High Holy Days. Jewish tradition says that God writes every person's words, deeds, and thoughts in the book of life, which he opens on Rosh HaShanah (for the book of life, see Ps. 69:28). If good deeds outnumber sinful ones for the year, that person's name will be inscribed in the book of life for another year on Yom Kippur. So during Rosh HaShanah and the Ten Days of Repentance, people can repent of their sins and do good deeds to increase their chances of being inscribed in the book of life.

Feast of Trumpets and Jesus

The apostle Paul writes that because of Christ's resurrection believers will be raised to eternal life at the trumpet's sound.

> We will not all sleep, but we will all be changed—in a flash,
> in the twinkling of an eye, at the last trumpet. For the
> trumpet will sound, the dead will be raised imperishable,
> and we will be changed.... Then the saying that is written
> will come true: "Death has been swallowed up in victory."
>
> 1 CORINTHIANS 15:51–54

Rosh HaShanah is sometimes referred to as the Day of Judgment. Jesus
said he has authority to judge all people (John 5:24–27). Paul called Jesus
the judge of "the living and the dead" (2 Tim. 4:1). God does have a book of
life: the Lamb's book of life (Rev. 21:27). However, doing good works does
not get one's name written in this book (Titus 3:5–7). The only way to have
one's name inscribed in the book is through faith in Jesus Christ as Savior.

Fascinating Facts about the Feast of Trumpets

✠ Nowadays, prior to Rosh HaShanah the shofar (ram's horn) is
blown to call people to repent and remind them that the holy days
are arriving.

✠ The shofar is blown one hundred times during Rosh HaShanah
synagogue services.

✠ For many, Rosh HaShanah is observed as a serious New Year's
holiday, not a happy one like January 1.

✠ A common custom is sending cards to relatives and friends to wish
them a happy, healthy, and prosperous new year. The message
includes the greeting *L'shanah tovah tikatevoo*,
which means "May you be inscribed [in
the book of life] for a good year."

✠ It is traditional to eat apple
slices dipped in honey. The
apples represent provision
and honey the sweetness
for the coming year.

DAY OF ATONEMENT

On the Day of Atonement, the high priest made atonement for sin in the Most Holy Place of the tabernacle (or later the temple). The Day of Atonement was the most solemn holy day of the year, a time for fasting and prayer.

> Do not do any work on that day, because it is the Day of Atonement, when atonement is made for you before the LORD your God.
>
> LEVITICUS 23:28

The Day of Atonement is called Yom Kippur. In Hebrew, *yom* means "day" and *kippur* means "atonement" or "covering." Atonement is God's way to bring reconciliation and restoration to the problem of human sin and its effects.

In Bible times, the high priest brought two animals, usually goats, to the tabernacle. He sacrificed one of the animals and offered the blood as a sacrifice of atonement on behalf of the people. This was an animal

The scapegoat

sacrifice to pay for his sins and the sins of the people. Then the high priest placed his hands on the other goat's head. He prayed, asking for God's forgiveness for all the sins of the people, and their sins were transferred onto the goat. Then the animal was released into the wilderness. This "scapegoat" carried Israel's sins far away (Lev. 16:1–34).

The Day of Atonement and Jesus

Christ came as high priest and entered the Most Holy Place once and for all, by his own blood, having obtained eternal redemption (Heb. 9:12). A thick curtain from floor to ceiling separated the Most Holy Place in the temple from the other rooms. When Jesus died on the cross, the curtain was ripped from top to bottom. Believers in Jesus accept his sacrifice on the cross as the final atonement for sin.

> But now he has appeared once for all at the culmination of the ages to do away with sin by the sacrifice of himself. Just as people are destined to die once, and after that to face judgment, so Christ was sacrificed once to take away the sins of many; and he will appear a second time, not to bear sin, but to bring salvation to those who are waiting for him.
>
> HEBREWS 9:26–28

Fascinating Facts about the Day of Atonement

✠ Today, the ten days between Rosh HaShanah and Yom Kippur are known as the Days of Repentance. Yom Kippur is considered the day when God judges people.

✠ Yom Kippur is a day of fasting, and no work is done on this day, including at home.

✠ Many Jewish people spend the day at synagogue, praying for forgiveness of their sins.

✠ The book of Jonah is read during the afternoon service to remind people of God's forgiveness and mercy.

✠ Immediately after the evening service, participants have a "breakfast" meal.

FEAST OF BOOTHS

The Feast of Booths was a reminder of Israel's forty-year wilderness wanderings. It was a way to remember God's faithfulness and protection during their journey when they dwelt in temporary shelters, or booths. During this holiday, the Israelites were to build and dwell in these shelters for seven days.

> Live in temporary shelters for seven days: All native-born Israelites are to live in such shelters so your descendants will know that I had the Israelites live in temporary shelters when I brought them out of Egypt.
>
> LEVITICUS 23:42–43

God required three things to be done for the Feast of Booths:

✠ Gather branches (or fruit) from palm, willow, and other trees (Lev. 23:40).

✠ Rejoice before the Lord (Deut. 16:13–14; Lev. 23:40).

✠ Live in booths (Lev. 23:42).

The Feast of Booths can also represent the final harvest when all nations will share in the joy and blessings of God's kingdom. Then all will celebrate this feast.

> Then the survivors from all the nations that have attacked Jerusalem will go up year after year to worship the King, the LORD Almighty, and to celebrate the Festival of Tabernacles [Booths].
>
> ZECHARIAH 14:16

The Feast of Booths and Jesus

By the time of Jesus, two ceremonies had been added to the last day of the festival in Jerusalem:

1. A priest would bring water from the pool of Siloam to the temple, symbolizing that when the Messiah comes the whole earth will know God "as the waters cover the sea" (Isa. 11:9).

2. People would carry torches and march around the temple, then set these lights around the walls of the temple, symbolizing how the Messiah would be a light to the gentiles.

When Jesus attended this festival (John 7:2), he said on the last day,

> Let anyone who is thirsty, come to me and drink. Whoever believes in me ... rivers of living water will flow from within them.
>
> JOHN 7:37–38

The next morning, while the torches were still burning, he said,

> I am the light of the world. Whoever follows me will never walk in darkness, but will have the light of life.
>
> JOHN 8:12

Fascinating Facts about the Feast of Booths

✠ The Feast of Booths is known as the Feast of Tabernacles or Sukkot, the Hebrew word for "booths."

✠ Jews continue to celebrate Sukkot by building temporary booths for eight days. Sukkot is a joyous festival when people rejoice in God's forgiveness and material blessings.

✠ The sukkah ("booth") is a temporary structure built of wood, or wood and canvas, and is usually erected on a lawn or balcony. It is decorated with fall flowers, leaves, fruits, and vegetables. Often at least one meal a day is eaten in the sukkah.

✠ The lulav is a bouquet made of palm, myrtle, and willow branches that are bound together and waved (or shaken) in praise to the Lord. The lulav is waved in all four directions (north, south, east, and west) and up and down to symbolize that God's presence is everywhere.

A modern sukkah

CHAPTER 7

The Ten Commandments: Then & Now

The Ten Commandments are the code of law given by God directly to Moses on Mount Sinai. After the exodus, God's chosen people almost immediately lost sight of his power and goodness to them. They resented their hardships and began to complain. They became quarrelsome and difficult to govern. Moses sought God's help on Mount Sinai. God himself engraved his will for the people on two tablets of stone.

✠ The first group of commandments laid out the rules to protect the harmony between God and people (commandments 1–4).

✠ The second group was designed to maintain respect between people (commandments 5–10).

The law was a gift from the God of Israel to his people. Unlike the other ancient near eastern gods, the Lord revealed his will and made it clear how to please him and how to properly conduct one's life in his community. God's law was vital to the stability of the forming tribal nation.

Disobedience to God's commands risked the community's survival. When a person broke a commandment, he had to pay a penalty, repay the person he had injured, and make a sacrifice to restore peace with God.

Despite the gift of these divine commands, the people set up idols and worshiped them, they lied, and they stole from one another. Many of their leaders were corrupt, and they refused to honor God. Over the centuries that followed, the law was often forgotten, and the worship of the true God was abandoned. God sent prophets and called to the people. Sometimes they would return to God and be restored. Other times, they would ignore him and suffer devastating hardships.

The Lord said that someday he would send a Savior and would have a new covenant with his people. The law would be written on their hearts, not on stone tablets. They would do the right thing because they loved God.

The days are coming … when I will make a new covenant with the people of Israel and with the people of Judah. It will not be like the covenant I made with their ancestors when I took them by the hand to lead them out of Egypt, because they broke my covenant, though I was a husband to them…. This is the covenant I will make with the people of Israel after that time…. I will put my law in their minds and write it on their hearts. I will be their God, and they will be my people."

JEREMIAH 31:31–33

God sent a Savior, Jesus Christ, to live a perfect life and take the penalty for sin through his death on the cross. Through his sacrifice, he made forgiveness and friendship with God possible, and made us perfect in God's eyes through faith. Jesus came to fulfill the law (Matt. 5:17–20).

This is how we know that we love the children of God: by loving God and carrying out his commands. In fact, this is love for God: to keep his commands. And his commands are not burdensome.

1 JOHN 5:2–3

HARMONY WITH GOD	HARMONY WITH OTHERS
1. No other gods	5. Honor parents
2. No idols	6. No murder
3. No misusing God's name	7. No adultery
4. Remember the Sabbath	8. No stealing
	9. No false testimony
	10. No covetousness

THE TEN COMMANDMENTS
Exodus 20:2–17

I am the LORD your God, who brought you out of Egypt, out of the land of slavery.

1 You shall have no other gods before me.

2 You shall not make for yourself an image in the form of anything in heaven above or on the earth beneath or in the waters below. You shall not bow down to them or worship them; for I, the LORD your God, am a jealous God, punishing the children for the sin of the parents to the third and fourth generation of those who hate me, but showing love to a thousand generations of those who love me and keep my commandments.

3 You shall not misuse the name of the LORD your God, for the LORD will not hold anyone guiltless who misuses his name.

4 Remember the Sabbath day by keeping it holy. Six days you shall labor and do all your work, but the seventh day is a Sabbath to the LORD your God. On it you shall not do any work, neither you, nor your son or daughter, nor your male or female servant, nor your animals, nor any foreigner residing in your towns. For in six days the LORD made the heavens and the earth, the sea, and all that is in them, but he rested on the seventh day. Therefore the LORD blessed the Sabbath day and made it holy.

5 Honor your father and your mother, so that you may live long in the land the LORD your God is giving you.

6 You shall not murder.

7 You shall not commit adultery.

8 You shall not steal.

9 You shall not give false testimony against your neighbor.

10 You shall not covet your neighbor's house. You shall not covet your neighbor's wife, or his male or female servant, his ox or donkey, or anything that belongs to your neighbor.

1. YOU SHALL HAVE NO OTHER GODS BEFORE ME.

MAIN IDEA: God is the creator and Lord of the universe, and he deserves our first loyalty.

Old Testament

✠ Abraham proved that God was his first priority by even being willing to give up his own son when God told him to (Gen. 22:1–14).

✠ The Israelites were worshiping other gods, so the prophet Elijah challenged the prophets of those gods to a contest. Elijah prayed that God would answer him so all would know that the Lord is God. The Lord answered with fire from heaven and proved his superiority (1 Kings 18:20–40).

✠ God commanded the prophet Hosea to marry an unfaithful woman as an illustration of how God feels when the people whom he loves turn to other gods (Hos. 1:2).

✠ In Babylon, Daniel and his three friends (Shadrach, Meshach, and Abednego) risked their lives because they remained devoted to the Lord as their only God and would bow down to him alone (Dan. 1; 3; 6).

New Testament

✠ When asked, "Which is the greatest commandment in the Law?" Jesus replied, "Love the Lord your God with all your heart and with all your soul and with all your mind. This is the first and greatest commandment" (Matt. 22:34–38).

✠ In the Sermon on the Mount, Jesus said, "No one can serve two masters. Either you will hate the one and love the other, or you will be devoted to the one and despise the other. You cannot serve both God and money" (Matt. 6:24).

✠ Jesus said, "Worship the Lord your God, and serve him only" (Luke 4:8).

Now

Put God first and give him your devotion. God should always be our highest priority, over everyone and everything. A "god" is anything that a person allows to rule his or her life. Other gods could include deities of other religions, superstitions, horoscopes, money, possessions, careers, personal comfort, family, friends, addictions, fame, power, security, romance, sex, church, a nation—anything that comes before the true God.

2. YOU SHALL NOT MAKE FOR YOURSELF AN IDOL.

MAIN IDEA: God is spirit, and he is greater than any representation.

Old Testament

✠ God gave many people the gift of craftsmanship and the skill to make beautiful things for the tabernacle and temple (Ex. 25:1–27:21; 1 Kings 7:23–26). To sculpt, paint, or design can bring glory to God. Yet God is spirit and cannot be represented by any image crafted by human hands. To do so would be an insult to the very nature of God.

✠ While Moses was on Mount Sinai receiving the Ten Commandments, the Israelites were busy making a golden calf idol. They bowed down and sacrificed offerings to it, angering God greatly (Ex.32:1–24).

✠ Gideon made an idol which became a snare for his family because Israel worshiped the idol instead of God (Judg. 8:26–27).

✠ The prophet Habakkuk said worshiping an idol is trusting in one's own creation—a lifeless, useless item (Hab. 2:18–19).

✠ The prophet Isaiah spoke of the foolishness of idol worship, saying that a person will burn a tree for warmth or cooking while using the same tree to fashion an idol for worship (Isa. 44:9–20).

New Testament

✠ When the Samaritan woman at the well met Jesus, she asked him whether people should worship God in Jerusalem or Samaria. He replied, "A time is coming and has now come when the true worshipers will worship the Father in Spirit and in truth, for they are the kind of worshipers the Father seeks. God is spirit, and his worshipers must worship in the Spirit and in truth" (John 4:23–24).

✠ The apostle Paul associated idolatry with impurity, lust, evil desires, and greed (Col. 3:5).

Now

Put your faith in God only. Idol worship is serving anything in the place of God. Idolatry can include the worship of the true God through an idol. God does not forbid or condemn all representations of people and animals, for he commanded in Scripture that ornamental artwork be made. But when we worship something we can see, touch, or control, we miss the power and grandeur of God.

The adoration of the golden calf

3. YOU SHALL NOT MISUSE THE NAME OF THE LORD.

MAIN IDEA: God's name is holy, powerful, and glorious.

Old Testament

✠ When a man named Shelomith blasphemed the name of God with a curse, the Lord commanded that he be taken outside the camp and stoned to death (Lev. 24:10–16).

✠ Any so-called prophet who claimed to speak in the name of God but did not actually receive a message from God was to be put to death (Deut. 18:20).

New Testament

✠ Jesus taught his disciples to begin prayers with, "Our Father in heaven, hallowed be your name" (Matt. 6:9).

✠ Jesus said, "Every kind of sin and slander can be forgiven, but blasphemy against the Spirit will not be forgiven…. But I tell you that everyone will have to give account on the day of judgment for every empty word they have spoken. For by your words you will be acquitted, and by your words you will be condemned" (Matt. 12:31, 36–37).

✠ The high priest said that Jesus broke the third commandment by claiming to be God, and he condemned Jesus to death for blasphemy (Matt. 26:62–66).

✠ The New Testament says that believers should pray, heal, and baptize in Jesus's name (Matt. 28:19; Mark 16:17; John 14:13; 16:23; Acts 3:6).

✠ God's command to us is to believe in the name of his Son, Jesus Christ (1 John 3:23).

Now

If we can show respect for the names of our fathers, mothers, teachers, and doctors, then how much more should we respect the name of our sovereign God. His name is holy and should be treated with respect. There is power in the Lord's name, and it should not be used lightly. James warns believers to watch what they say because the tongue is capable of evil and poison, and it can easily corrupt a person (James 3:5–9). As God's creation, everything a person says and does should be done in order to praise and glorify God (1 Cor. 10:31).

4. REMEMBER THE SABBATH DAY.

MAIN IDEA: God values rest, spiritual refreshment, and time for his people to worship him.

Old Testament

✠ The Sabbath was ordained in creation, for God rested on the seventh day after creating the universe (Gen. 2:2–3).

✠ The Sabbath was ordered by God just after the exodus, but before the Ten Commandments were given (Ex. 16:23–29).

✠ Death was the prescribed punishment for working on the Sabbath (Ex. 35:2–3).

✠ Every fiftieth year in Israel was to be a sabbath year, the Year of Jubilee, in which the land would not be tilled, slaves were freed, and alienated property restored (Lev. 25:8–33).

✠ The prophet Isaiah wrote that God detested meaningless sacrifices and empty obedience to religious festivals, to new moon celebrations, and even to the Sabbath day (Isa. 1:11–13).

New Testament

✠ When Jesus started healing people on the Sabbath, the synagogue ruler told the people to leave and come back to be healed on any other day but the Sabbath. The ruler thought that healing on the Sabbath was a violation of the fourth commandment. Jesus rebuked him and told the people that it is acceptable to do acts of mercy, even on the Sabbath (Luke 13:10–17).

✠ Jesus said, "The Sabbath was made for man, not man for the Sabbath. So the Son of Man is Lord even of the Sabbath" (Mark 2:27–28).

✠ In the Old Testament, the Sabbath day was observed on Saturday, the seventh day of the week. Jesus rose from the dead on Sunday morning, the first day of the week. Since then, most believers have observed Sunday as "the Lord's day" on which tithes are given and the Lord's Supper (Communion) is celebrated (Acts 20:7; 1 Cor. 16:1–2; Rev. 1:10).

Now

Many Christians observe the Sabbath on Sunday and see it as a holy day to rest, refocus, and praise God for creating us anew in Christ. Others believe that the Sabbath should still take place on Saturday, and some do not observe the Sabbath but rather see all days as holy.

In the Old Testament, God gave his people a day of rest after six days of labor. He knew how to preserve his creation, and rest was a necessary component to that preservation. Without rest, valuable topsoil is used up

and the land becomes useless. In the same way, without rest, human beings become unproductive. Without spiritual refreshment, we can have rested bodies inhabited by unrested minds.

The very center of Sabbath rest is the worship of God. Worship is where human beings find fulfillment because it is what we were made for. The Sabbath day, or any period of rest, can serve as an opportunity to renew our relationship with God and refocus our attention on him.

5. HONOR YOUR FATHER AND YOUR MOTHER.

MAIN IDEA: God wants all people to respect and honor their parents.

Old Testament

✠ The Old Testament strictly warns children against cursing and abusing their parents (Ex. 21:15, 17).

✠ The book of Proverbs says that wisdom comes from obeying one's parents (Prov. 23:22–25).

New Testament

✠ Jesus was obedient to his earthly parents as he grew up in Nazareth (Luke 2:51).

✠ Jesus rebuked the Jewish authorities of his day for not taking care of their aging parents. He said that they made up excuses in order to avoid having to honor their parents (Matt. 15:4–6).

✠ Jesus taught that he must be a priority even above one's family: "Anyone who loves their father or mother more than me is not worthy of me; anyone who loves their son or daughter more than me is not worthy of me" (Matt. 10:37).

✠ Jesus honored his mother by ensuring that she was cared for once he was gone (John 19:26–27).

✠ The apostle Paul commanded children to obey their parents in everything, and he reminded them that the fifth commandment contained a promise: if children honor their parents, they will enjoy a long life (Eph. 6:1–3; Col. 3:20).

Now

The Hebrew word *kabed* means "to make honorable" or "to glorify." This verb has a wide range of connotations that far exceeds simple obedience.

It is important to obey parents, but children must also show their parents honor.

Sometimes we must follow God instead of obeying our parents. God's will is more important than the will of one's parents. When parents command or model something that is against God's will or goes against loving God and others, they can still be shown honor without being obeyed.

We should treat parents with respect, no matter what the situation may be. Most parents made great sacrifices to bring up their children. No one is a perfect parent, and in some cases, fathers and mothers are dishonorable and have caused pain and grief. Even in these cases, when parents may not deserve it, God expects us to honor them for his sake. God promises long life to those who honor their parents.

6. YOU SHALL NOT MURDER.

MAIN IDEA: God created human life and holds it sacred.

Old Testament

✠ The first murder in the Bible was committed by Cain who killed his brother Abel out of jealousy (Gen. 4:1–16).

✠ After the flood, God told Noah, "Whoever sheds human blood, by humans shall their blood be shed; for in the image of God has God made mankind" (Gen. 9:6).

✠ Old Testament men like Simeon, Levi, Moses, Joab, David, and Absalom were all guilty of murder (Gen. 49:5–7; Ex. 2:11–12; 2 Sam. 3:27; 11:14–15; 13:28).

✠ The Bible says that God hates and detests hands that shed innocent blood (Prov. 6:16–17).

New Testament

- ✠ Jesus taught, "You have heard that it was said to the people long ago, 'You shall not murder, and anyone who murders will be subject to judgment.' But I tell you that anyone who is angry with his brother or sister will be subject to judgment" (Matt. 5:21–22).

- ✠ The apostle Paul encouraged the believers in Rome to live at peace with everyone and reminded them that revenge belongs only to God (Rom. 12:18–19).

- ✠ The apostle John wrote that anyone who hates his brother is a murderer. He also wrote that true love is evident in those who lay down their lives for others (1 John 3:15–16).

Now

Murder is the unlawful killing of another human being, usually premeditated. The Hebrew word *ratsach*, always translated as "murder," is used for this sixth commandment to contrast this prohibition with other forms of killing such as accidental death, war, self-defense, capital punishment, and the killing of animals. God created human beings in his own image. To take another's life is to destroy the image of God. As with the breaking of the other commandments, murder ultimately comes from the heart.

7. YOU SHALL NOT COMMIT ADULTERY.

MAIN IDEA: God values faithfulness and sexual purity.

Old Testament

- ✠ According to Old Testament law, anyone who committed adultery should be put to death (Lev. 20:10).

- ✠ God compared unfaithfulness to him with adultery, which is unfaithfulness to the marriage covenant (Jer. 3:6–9).

✠ After King David committed adultery with Bathsheba, the wife of Uriah, the prophet Nathan confronted him for his sin. David confessed and wrote Psalm 51, a psalm of repentance: "Create in me a pure heart, O God, and renew a steadfast spirit within me. Do not cast me from your presence or take your Holy Spirit from me" (Ps. 51:10–11).

New Testament

✠ In the Sermon on the Mount, Jesus taught, "You have heard that it was said, 'You shall not commit adultery.' But I tell you that anyone who looks at a woman lustfully has already committed adultery with her in his heart" (Matt. 5:27–28).

✠ Jesus also said, "I tell you that anyone who divorces his wife, except for sexual immorality, and marries another woman commits adultery" (Matt. 19:9; see also Matt. 5:31–32).

✠ Jesus forgave a woman who had been caught in adultery. He told her that no one condemned her and to go and sin no more (John 8:10–11).

Now

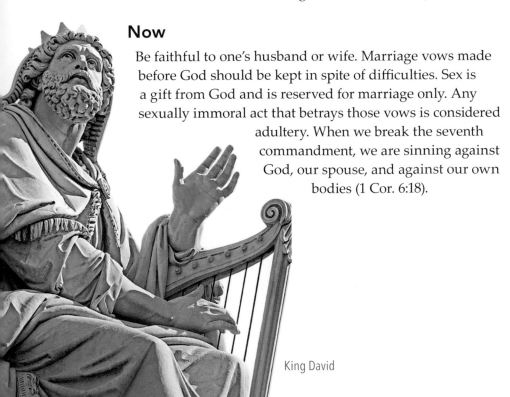

Be faithful to one's husband or wife. Marriage vows made before God should be kept in spite of difficulties. Sex is a gift from God and is reserved for marriage only. Any sexually immoral act that betrays those vows is considered adultery. When we break the seventh commandment, we are sinning against God, our spouse, and against our own bodies (1 Cor. 6:18).

King David

8. YOU SHALL NOT STEAL.

MAIN IDEA: God values productivity, integrity, and generosity.

Old Testament

✠ The book of Proverbs says that engaging in things like fraud, theft, and extortion will lead to one's own ruin (Prov. 20:17; 24:15–16; 28:16).

✠ Proverbs also says that people should pay their debts and warns against the dangers of defaulting on loans and neglecting bills (Prov. 22:26–27).

✠ The prophet Malachi said that when people do not bring their full tithe and offering to God, they are stealing from God. But God promises to bless those who bring him the full amount (Mal. 3:8–12).

New Testament

✠ In the Sermon on the Mount, Jesus taught that we can trust our heavenly Father to provide for our needs: "Do not worry about your life, what you will eat or drink; or about your body, what you will wear. Is not life more than food, and the body more than clothes? Look at the birds of the air; they do not sow or reap or store away in barns, and yet your heavenly Father feeds them. Are you not much more valuable than they?" (Matt. 6:25–26).

✠ Jesus also taught generosity: "If anyone wants to sue you and take your shirt, hand over your coat as well.… Give to the one who asks you, and do not turn away from the one who wants to borrow from you" (Matt. 5:40–42).

✠ The apostle Paul wrote to the Ephesians telling them to stop stealing and to start working for their money, so that they could share with the needy (Eph. 4:28).

Now

In the kingdom of God that Jesus describes, people give freely and allow others to borrow things from them without asking anything in return. Jesus presents a picture of a caring kingdom, a kingdom where people give to others out of love. In such an environment, there would be no need for stealing because of lack of food, clothing, or shelter. Additionally, there would be no need for loans or debt because peoples' needs are cared for by one another. Christians in the book of Acts expressed these principles in how they cared for each other (Acts 4:32–37). This kind of honesty and generosity among believers is what the church today is still called to embody.

9. YOU SHALL NOT GIVE FALSE TESTIMONY.

MAIN IDEA: God is truth and he values honesty.

Old Testament

✠ According to Old Testament law, if a witness who accused someone of a crime was proven to be maliciously lying, then the punishment that the defendant would have received should be given to the false witness (Deut. 19:16–20).

✠ Proverbs says that wise people keep falsehoods far from them (Prov. 30:8); God hates a lying tongue but delights in those who tell the truth (Prov. 12:22); and those who speak the truth are trustworthy and are valued by rulers (Prov. 16:13).

New Testament

✠ Jesus said that "everyone will have to give account on the day of judgment for every empty word they have spoken. For by your words you will be acquitted, and by your words you will be condemned" (Matt. 12:36–37).

✠ Jesus said that he is the truth: "I am the way and the truth and the life. No one comes to the Father except through me" (John 14:6).

✠ In the early church, Ananias and Sapphira sold some property and claimed to donate the entire amount to the church. Instead, they kept part of the money for themselves. The apostle Peter said they were free to keep some of the money, but because they falsely claimed to give the entire amount, they lied to the Holy Spirit. Their lie resulted in immediate death by the hand of God (Acts 5:1–11).

Now

People who tell the truth can be trusted, but liars cannot. Even when a liar does tell the truth, he or she may not be believed because of their past lies. Truth-telling makes for a functional and just society. Respectful honesty and truth nurture relationships and help foster communities that are enriching. Be trustworthy and maintain integrity by being honest. Lying can take the form of gossip, false accusations, blame shifting, and even self-deceit. It is important to keep promises and be responsible for the commitments we make.

Ananias and Sapphira

10. YOU SHALL NOT COVET.

MAIN IDEA: God values humility, contentment, and peace.

Old Testament

✠ King Saul was jealous of David's success and coveted the respect and praise David received from the women in all the towns (1 Sam. 18:6–9).

✠ King David coveted his neighbor's wife, Bathsheba. David then murdered Bathsheba's husband to cover up his treachery (2 Sam. 11:1–27).

✠ Proverbs says that envy "rots the bones" but contentment gives life (Prov. 14:30).

New Testament

✠ In the Sermon on the Mount, Jesus taught: "Do not worry, saying, 'What shall we eat?' or 'What shall we drink?' or 'What shall we wear?' For the pagans run after all these things, and your heavenly Father knows that you need them. But seek first his kingdom and his righteousness, and all these things will be given to you as well" (Matt. 6:31–33).

✠ Jesus said that a person's life does not consist in the abundance of possessions (Luke 12:15).

✠ A rich young man with a lifelong commitment to keeping all the commandments came to Jesus and asked what more he needed to do. Jesus's response to him went right to the heart of the tenth commandment: "One thing you lack.… Go, sell everything you have and give to the poor, and you will have treasure in heaven. Then come, follow me" (Mark 10:17–23).

✠ The apostle Paul encouraged believers to be content with what they had and warned them about loving money and possessions. He said that the love of money is a root of all kinds of evil; it causes greed, envy, and pride (Phil. 4:11–12; 1 Tim. 6:6–10).

✠ The apostle John warned believers about loving the world and the things of the world. He said that those who love the world do not have the love of God in them (1 John 2:15).

Now

God wants us to be content with what we have and to keep our eyes focused on him; not on the things of this world. Be content and do not long for things that belong to others. Avoid the pursuit of happiness and joy through the accumulation of material wealth, possessions, or someone else's spouse or another's friends and social status. Do not allow earthly things to fill a void that only God can fill. Ask God to provide; he promises that he will take care of our needs if we seek him first.

WHICH IS THE MOST IMPORTANT COMMANDMENT?

When the Pharisees asked Jesus which commandment in the law was the greatest, he said:

> "Love the Lord your God with all your heart and with all your soul and with all your mind." This is the first and greatest commandment. And the second is like it: "Love your neighbor as yourself." All the Law and the Prophets hang on these two commandments.
>
> MATTHEW 22:37–40

All the commandments and rules in the Bible can be summed up under two basic principles:

✠ Love God with your whole self.

✠ Love your neighbor as yourself.

Every law is based on a principle. In Jesus's day, many people were obeying the law, but they were not upholding God's principles. Jesus told the parable of the Good Samaritan to illustrate this point (Luke 10:25–37). In the story, a man is attacked on a road and left for dead. A priest and a then Levite (people who would have known the law very well) pass by the man and do not help him. Later, a Samaritan (considered to be a lower-class person) comes across the injured man and helps him. The Samaritan even pays for the man's medical treatment.

The religious law did not allow anyone to touch a dead body. Even though this man was not dead, he may have appeared dead to those walking by. The Samaritan risked disobeying the law in order to show mercy to an injured man. The priest and the Levite passed by the man for fear of breaking this law.

For Jesus, showing mercy to others and truly loving your neighbor is far more important than obeying a religious purity law. Jesus encouraged people to live by the spirit of the law rather than the letter of the law. He wanted people to make sure they understood why we obey a commandment.

Paul said that with Christ the law is no longer written on tablets of stone, but it is written on our hearts (2 Cor. 3:1–17). The reason we break a commandment stems from what is in our hearts. In the same way, the reason we obey a commandment is because our hearts have been transformed in Christ.

PHOTOS AND ILLUSTRATIONS

Images used under license from Shutterstock.com: cover: Dmitry Rukhlenko (caravan), Rocksweeper (sea parted), Guenter Albers (pyramids), ChameleonsEye (pharaoh), KPegg (tabernacle); backgrounds and borders: Ashwin, Jacob_09; p. 7 DKR design; p. 12 Fresco of Moses and the Pharaoh, Altlerchenfelder church, Vienna, photo by Renata Sedmakova; p. 13 Cyril PAPOT (Temple); p. Simon Vasut (frog); p. 14 Malago (gnats), Fawwaz Media (flies), Andrea Izzotti (Sekhmet), Tomb QV66 Queen Nefertari, Luxor, Egypt, photo by Kirk Fisher (Kherpi); p. 15 krengkamon (hail), Dark_Side (locust), Dudarev Mikhail (pyramids), Stephen Chung (horus), Evgeni ShouldRa and Paul Vinten (blood, doorframe); p. 18 Lotus_studio; p. 23 Zeteo Theos Photography; p. 26 ArtMari; p. 34-37 givaga; p. 52 Kenneth Keifer (crosses), photo by Renata Sedmakova (God shows Abraham stars); p. 73 Death of Korah, photo by Nicku; p. 74 Dance60; p. 76 Franck Legros (Ramses II on display in Paris); p. 87 ChameleonsEye; p. 88 xpixel (ash), Olga_Shestakova (grain), Philip Kinsey (lamb); p. 90 stockcreations; p. 95 aguilasdefuego; p. 98, 102 James Steidl; p. 100 RungnapaXIII15 (gold jar), SeDmi (branch); p. 101 jsp; p. 102 aguilasdefuego; (tabernacle); p. 103 LittlePerfectStock (wise men); p. 105 ImageBank4u; p. 112 brillianticon (lamb), ArtMari; p. 114 Brian Minkoff (Seder plate); p. 115 BesticonPark; p. 116 Pixel-Shot; p. 117 Tribalium; p. 118 Didecs; p. 119 Wiktoria Matynia; p. 120 vetre; p. 121 Fox Design (icon), John Theodor; p. 122 Kovaleva_Ka; p. 125 tomertu; p. 127 alefbet; p. 130 Zvonimir Atletic; p. 132 Corax_Cole; p. 133 Janon Stock; p. 134 Marcus_Hofmann; p. 136 Anastazzo; p. 137 Love You Stock; p. 138 d.ee_angelo; p. 139 BigPixel Photo; p. 140 ArtMari; p. 141 Valentina Razumova; p. 142 zebra0209; p. 143 Pressmaster; p. 144 file404; p. 146 New Africa

Art: p. 10 Moses and the Burning Bush by Gebhard Fugel (1920); p. 14 Boils illustration in the Toggenburg Bible (1411); p. 17 The Destruction of Pharaoh's Army by Philippe Jacques de Loutherbourg II (1792); p. 52 The Expulsion of Adam and Eve from Paradise by Benjamin West (1791), National Gallery of Art; p. 52 Noah and His Ark by Charles Peale (c. 1819); p. 52 Moses before the Burning Bush by Domenico Fetti (c. 1613); p. 52 King David by Barbieri (c. 1651); p. 67 The Goldsmith by James Tissot (c. 1896–1902), The Jewish Museum; p. 70 Jethro Advising Moses by Jan van Bronchorst (1659); p. 71 Victory O Lord! by John Everett Millais (1871); p. 72 Moses and the Messengers from Canaan by Lanfranco (c. 1621); p. 77 Pharaoh's Daughter Finding Baby Moses by Flavitsky (1830–1866); p. 79 Moses Leaving for Egypt by Perugino (c. 1482); p. 102 The Ark Passes Over the Jordan by James Tissot (c. 1896-1902), The Jewish Museum; p. 102 The Philistines Place the Ark of the Covenant in the Temple of Dagon by Battista Franco (c. 1540), The Metropolitan Museum of Art; p. 103 David Bearing the Ark of the Covenant into Jerusalem (16th century); p. 103 The Burning of Jerusalem (17th century); p. 108 The Songs of Joy by James Tissot (c. 1896–1902), The Jewish Museum; p. 123 The Scapegoat by William Hunt (1854); p. 135 The Adoration of the Golden Calf by Nicolas Poussin (1633)

Other: p. 15 Egyptian god Seth, Rama/Wikimedia; p. 27, 66 Moses and Aaron © 1989 by Robert Florczack in Tyndale Family Bible (Tyndale House Publishers, Inc.); p. 32 Amarna letter: Royal Letter from Abi-milku of Tyre to the king of Egypt, The Metropolitan Museum of Art; p. 33 Merneptah Stele, Webscribe/Wikimedia; p. 68 Caleb by Jeffrey Terreson in Tyndale Family Bible (Tyndale House Publishers, Inc.); p. 83 Tabernacle illustration by Cristalle Kishi/Rose Publishing; p. 104 Chapel of the Tablet A. Davey/Wikimedia; p. 145 Ananias and Sapphira on ivory casket (4th century)/Wikimedia. Tabernacle art by © Jerry Allison (p. 85, 86, 91, 94, 96, 97). Relief portions of maps by Michael Schmeling/www.aridocean.com.

ROSE VISUAL BIBLE STUDIES
6-Session Study Guides for Personal or Group Use

THE BOOK OF JAMES
Find out how to cultivate a living faith through six tests of faith.

THE TABERNACLE
Discover how each item of the tabernacle foreshadowed Jesus.

THE ARMOR OF GOD
Dig deep into Ephesians 6 and learn the meaning of each piece of the armor.

THE LIFE OF PAUL
See how the apostle Paul persevered through trials and proclaimed the gospel.

JOURNEY TO THE RESURRECTION
Renew your heart and mind as you engage in spiritual practices. Perfect for Easter.

I AM
Know the seven powerful claims of Christ from the gospel of John.

THE TWELVE DISCIPLES
Learn about the twelve men Jesus chose to be his disciples.

PROVERBS
Gain practical, godly wisdom from the book of Proverbs.

WOMEN OF THE BIBLE: OLD TESTAMENT
Journey through six inspiring stories of women of courage and wisdom.

WOMEN OF THE BIBLE: NEW TESTAMENT
See women's impact in the ministry of Jesus and the early church.

THE LORD'S PRAYER
Deepen your prayer life with the seven petitions in the Lord's Prayer.

FRUIT OF THE SPIRIT
Explore the nine spiritual fruits.

PSALMS
Discover the wild beauty of praise.

THE EXODUS
Witness God's mighty acts in the exodus.

THE BOOK OF JOB
Explore questions about faith and suffering.

www.hendricksonrose.com

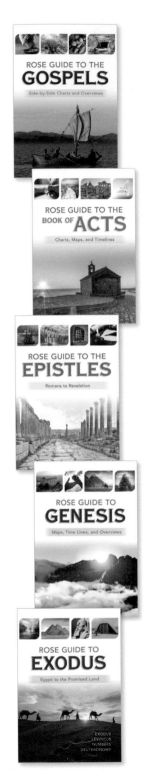

ROSE GUIDE TO THE GOSPELS

Includes: key information about the uniqueness of each gospel; a harmony of the gospels; who's who in the gospels; background to the world of Jesus; evidence for the resurrection.

ISBN 9781628628111

ROSE GUIDE TO THE BOOK OF ACTS

Includes: overview of the book of Acts; understanding the message and background of Acts; life of the apostle Paul; who's who in Acts; time line and maps; the Holy Spirit in the lives of Christians.

ISBN 9781649380203

ROSE GUIDE TO THE EPISTLES

Includes: overview of the epistles; key facts on each epistle at a glance; who's who in the epistles; the seven churches of Revelation; comparison of Christian views on the book of Revelation.

ISBN 9781649380227

ROSE GUIDE TO GENESIS

Includes: charts, maps, and time lines for the book of Genesis; stories of Noah's ark, Abraham, and Joseph; understanding the ancient world; who's who in Genesis.

ISBN 9781496477996

ROSE GUIDE TO EXODUS

Includes: life of Moses; when and where the exodus occurred; the tabernacle and the ark; Passover and other feasts; the Ten Commandments.

ISBN 9781496484598

www.hendricksonrose.com